DATE DUE			

PARLIAMENT AND FOREIGN AFFAIRS

Parliament
and Foreign Affairs

BY

PETER G. RICHARDS

Reader in Politics
University of Southampton

Toronto
UNIVERSITY OF TORONTO PRESS

TO
Diane Gwyneth

PREFACE

THIS book is an attempt to survey a problem of democratic institutions that has been curiously neglected for the past forty years. The number of detailed research studies now appearing on various aspects of the British Parliament is greater than ever before; but its function in relation to foreign policy has been ignored. I hope that the book may provide something of a bridge between the study of political institutions and the study of international politics. The British approach to our own institutions is excessively insular: far too little attention is paid to the role of the state in the international community. On the other hand, those who specialize in foreign affairs should perhaps consider more closely the problem of how public opinion can and should influence decision-making in a democracy.

No satisfactory examination of the political process can be made without assistance from those who are leading participants. I acknowledge with gratitude the help received from the Director of the Royal Institute of International Affairs, from Members of Parliament of all shades of opinion, from present or past members of the staffs of the House of Commons, the Foreign Office, the Conservative Party, the Labour Party and the Trades Union Congress.

My task was greatly facilitated by a term's sabbatical leave and I am grateful to my colleagues in the Department of Politics at Southampton who undertook my normal duties during this period. Professor J. Frankel has made many valuable suggestions on the work as also has Mr O'Sullivan. Miss Jill Boyle took much care over typing the first draft of the book. Mrs Anne Harris compiled the statistical material. Miss Diana Marshallsay, Librarian of the Ford Collection of Parliamentary Papers, has again given me invaluable aid by providing the Index.

My wife, as usual, has undertaken the toil of polishing the final version and preparing it for the printer.

PETER G. RICHARDS
University of Southampton
Christmas Eve, 1966

CONTENTS

CHAPTER I

Introduction

PARLIAMENT'S consideration of foreign affairs must differ substantially from the way in which it conducts other business. There are a number of reasons which reinforce the distinction. The essence of foreign policy is negotiation rather than legislation: negotiation may result in treaties or other international agreements, the parliamentary scrutiny of which is less detailed than that of legislation. As international negotiations require compromise with the interests of other states, their outcome is less under ministerial control than items of internal policy; inevitably this weakens the position of the legislature. Foreign issues have an element of remoteness and Members of Parliament may be less well informed about them, and since their constituents are more concerned with immediate social and economic issues, there is little popular pressure to induce backbenchers to concentrate on international problems. Save at times of great crisis, foreign policy tends to be overlaid by other issues. Debate is also restrained because often there is a consensus of view between the Government and Opposition. One other factor has also to be noted—the need for secrecy in foreign affairs. This has constantly been put forward as a reason for inhibiting parliamentary debate and provides Ministers with a useful screen against criticism. In fact, there is more pre-natal secrecy surrounding a Budget than there is over many international negotiations. However, foreign affairs are generally considered a matter for the executive branch of government: in Britain they have traditional associations, now greatly weakened, with the Royal Prerogative and the aristocracy.

This summary indicates that there are formidable difficulties to effective parliamentary examination of foreign affairs. Each item in the catalogue of obstacles will be examined in detail in the chapters which follow. But as a preliminary it is worth discussing why this aspect of Parliament's duties has not been examined before. There is a growing literature on the British Parliament and detailed analysis has been made of much of its procedure. But its role in foreign affairs is passed over. The subject gets sparse mention in the text-books on British Government and was accorded but a single chapter in the American study, D. G. Bishop's *The Administration of British Foreign Relations*.[1] The literature on the United States is much more fruitful.[2]

Why have British writers tended to ignore the role of their own Parliament in international matters? One factor may be that, until recently, the study of International Relations was poorly supported by British universities. Further, where the subject was pursued, work was carried on in university departments divorced from general studies in political science. It can well be argued that this is a particular demonstration of the general phenomenon of British insularity: that in spite of two world wars and our unique dependence on international trade, we have a sense of separateness and detachment which means we think we do not need to bother overmuch about the rest of the world. Such an attitude exists, to be sure—but not at the level of political consciousness of those who write and read books on political science. Probably the main reason is that those interested in parliamentary studies tend to feel that foreign affairs must be an unsatisfactory subject. In the nuclear age major issues must be settled, or left unsettled, by the major powers, the United States and the Soviet Union. At the time of the Cuba crisis the British Government had to stand by helplessly: even had Parliament been in session at the time, what could it have done? All of which is acutely frustrating for the democrat who wishes to see a reformed and envigorated Parliament providing both a better stimulus to, and a better reflection of, public opinion. So this aspect of parliament's work is put on one side with a suggestion that the Commons need a specialized committee to deal with foreign affairs.

[1] Syracuse University Press, 1961.

[2] R. A. Dahl, *Congress and Foreign Policy* (Harcourt Brace, 1950). H. N. Carroll, *The House of Representatives and Foreign Affairs* (University of Pittsburg, 1958). J. A. Robinson, *Congress and Foreign Policy Making* (Dorsey Press, 1962). M. E. Jewell, *Senatorial Politics and Foreign Policy* (University of Kentucky, 1962).

Introduction

It is now sometimes argued that foreign affairs has become a branch of defence policy; that it is dominated by the strategic demands of a potential conflict between the major power blocs. This view is surely too simple. Certainly the relationship between foreign affairs and defence is close, but it is not wholly unrealistic to argue that there are some political or even ethical principles in Britain's approach to international controversies. To separate Commonwealth and Colonial problems from foreign policy is even more difficult. The rather special issues associated with the granting of independence to dependent territories have been avoided except where, as in the case of Rhodesia, they have grown into matters of international dispute.

I have concentrated attention on the House of Commons since it is the dominant chamber of Parliament. References to 'Members' will always be to Members of the Commons. However, some account is also given of the debates of the noble lords in the Upper House.

This book is not intended to be an *exposé* of the weakness of Parliament. It accepts that institutional reform in Britain can do nothing to change the realities of the world situation. But it is intended to throw a spotlight on a neglected aspect of the British political process that continues to be of importance. There are still vital choices open to this country in the international field, especially in our future relations with Europe.

CHAPTER II

Popular Control of Foreign Policy

HISTORICAL RETROSPECT

DOUBTS about the ability of a legislature to deal with international questions and decisions about war and peace were first given powerful expression by John Locke. He named the function of dealing with foreign affairs as 'the federative power'.

'And though this *federative Power* in the well or ill management of it be of great moment to the commonwealth, yet it is much less capable to be directed by antecedent, standing, positive Laws, than the *Executive*; and so must necessarily be left to the Prudence and Wisdom of those whose hands it is in, to be managed for the publick good. For the Laws that concern Subjects one amongst another, being to direct their actions, may well enough precede them. But what is to be done in reference to *Foreigners*, depending much upon their actions, and the variation of designs and interests, must be *left* in great part *to* the *Prudence* of those who have this Power committed to them, to be managed by the best of their Skill, for the advantage of the Commonwealth.'[1]

Locke's argument is simply that the conduct of foreign affairs demands exceptional treatment as it does not require the passing of legislation to regulate subsequent conduct, but it does need immediate actions in response to events abroad. There is no doubt that this proposition has had great influence in Britain and elsewhere. But its connection with Locke's view of the Prerogative is less well remembered.[2] Locke was prepared for the executive to take action without legal authority, indeed to act contrary to the law if this were for the public good—a mediaeval standpoint that would have been opposed by any

[1] John Locke, *The Second Treatise of Government*, Ch. XII.
[2] *Ibid* Ch. XIV.

16

nineteenth-century democrat. But Locke was not a democrat. His claim was that government is founded on consent, that rulers—be they kings or legislatures—exercise a trust and that rebellion becomes justifiable if this trust be abused. For his contemporaries, Locke's attitude to foreign affairs was made more acceptable by our insular political situation. Britain had not yet become an Imperial Power: in terms of war and peace, the central fear was of invasion from the Continent. It therefore seemed certain that the 'federative power' would be used essentially for defensive purposes and not in an arbitrary or aggressive way.

The framers of the United States Constitution, being more concerned to reduce the probability of misuse of power by institutional checks, failed to follow Locke's guidance. Instead they insisted that treaties should be made by the President by and with the advice and consent of the Senate and provided that two-thirds of the Senators present agreed. On this stipulation *The Federalist*[1] commented with satisfaction: 'Thus we see that the Constitution provides that our negotiations for treaties shall have every advantage that can be derived from talents, information, integrity and deliberate investigations on the one hand, and from secrecy and despatch on the other.' Further, the responsibility for declaring war was placed upon the Congress, and the Presidential nomination of ambassadors was subject to Senatorial approval. There is little sign here of willingness to trust the discretion of the executive. Half a century later de Tocqueville surveyed the working of American government and found much to admire, but he was dubious of its competence in foreign affairs.

'Foreign politics demand scarcely any of those qualities which a democracy possesses; and they require, on the contrary, the perfect use of almost all those faculties in which it is deficient. Democracy is favourable to the increase of the internal resources of the State; it tends to diffuse a moderate independence; it promotes the growth of public spirit, and fortifies the respect which is entertained for law in all classes of society; and these are advantages which only exercise an indirect influence over the relations which one people bears to another. But a democ-

[1] No. LXIV.

racy is unable to regulate the details of an important undertaking, to persevere in a design, and to work out its execution in the presence of serious obstacles. It cannot combine its measures with secrecy, and it will not await their consequences with patience.'[1]

The need for secrecy has been a regular obsession with British Governments, but the idea that a democracy may be devoid of a sense of national purpose in face of difficulty is perhaps now more acceptable across the North Atlantic than it is here.[2]

The concept of popular control of foreign policy is open to varying interpretation. It may mean that the conduct of foreign relations should be subject to the approval of a legislature, or it may imply that everyone should be able to influence decisions. Those who advocate the former need not necessarily support the latter: the Founding Fathers of the United States would have been horrified by the idea that the treaty making power should be exercised only subject to the wishes of a majority of the whole population. Clearly, a number of factors influence the strength of the check to executive authority—the constitutional powers of the legislature, the independence of spirit of the legislature, the extent of the franchise and the vigour of public opinion. It is notable that while these factors change in strength, the movements are not necessarily in a uniform direction. Thus in mid-nineteenth century Britain the influence of the House of Commons over foreign affairs reached its peak, although British political life was less democratic than it is to-day. The Commons discussed the subject at will and the amount of time devoted to it varied with the degree of international tension.[3] Major debates were initiated by backbench Members, e.g. the Don Pacifico debate in 1850 and the 1855 motion for an enquiry

[1] Alexis de Tocqueville, *Democracy in America*, (The World's Classics, O.U.P.), p. 161.

[2] Walter Lippmann has argued that popular control weakens foreign policy because 'the pressure of the electorate is normally on the soft side of the equations': *The Public Philosophy* (Hamish Hamilton, 1955), p. 47. See also H. J. Morgenthau, *In Defence of the National Interest* (Knopf, 1951), p. 223.

[3] A year by year analysis of the proportion of parliamentary time spent on foreign affairs is given by A. C. Turner in *The House of Commons and Foreign Policy 1830–67*, a thesis in the Bodleian.

into the Crimean War. Governments were fearful not of the electorate, but of parliamentary opinion; between 1835 and 1874 each Cabinet was defeated by the House of Commons, not at the polls. In 1857 the Government was defeated over the China War. Britain's failure to intervene in the Schleswig crisis of 1864 was due mainly to the pressure of parliamentary opinion.[1]

In mid-Victorian England Radicals gave but intermittent attention to foreign affairs. Cobden and Bright argued that wars and international crises were due to the machinations of the aristocracy which attempted to inhibit public discussion.[2] When states became democratic disputes could be settled by more civilized methods of arbitration. Foreign affairs deflected attention from internal social and economic problems: international crises were sometimes convenient for governments as they encouraged patriotic sentiments and diverted men's minds from domestic grievances. Thus Radical opinion looked upon foreign policy with distaste and tended to avoid the subject, with some major exceptions including the welcome given to Kossuth in 1851. The attitude of detachment was strengthened by Britain's insular position and the strength of the Navy which removed any fear of invasion. It was also a period in which Europe was mercifully free from any major clash of arms; instead there was a surge of popular movements striving to throw off foreign or aristocratic dominance. Other conflicts in Asia and Africa were remote and of minor consequence to everday life. A diverse and vigorous Press, combined with a Commons in which Members often acted independently of

[1] A. J. P. Taylor, *The Troublemakers* (Hamish Hamilton, 1957), pp. 65–6.

[2] 'When you come to our foreign policy, you are no longer Englishmen, you are no longer free; you are recommended not to inquire. If you do you are told you cannot understand it; you are snubbed, you are hustled aside. We are told that the matter is too deep for common understandings like ours—that there is a great mystery about it. We have what is called diplomacy. We have a great many lords engaged in what they call diplomacy. We have a lord in Paris, we have another in Madrid, another in Berlin, another in Vienna, and another lord in Constantinople; we have another at Washington—in fact, almost all over the world, particularly where the society is most pleasant and the climate most agreeable, there is almost certain to be an English nobleman to represent the English Foreign Office, but you never know what he is doing'. *Speeches by John Bright*, ed. J. E. Thorold Rogers (Macmillan, 1869), Vol. II, pp. 75–6.

party, ensured that opinion was flexible. Every Foreign Secretary since Castlereagh had been conscious of the importance of informed opinion, and some had led opinion with care and skill. In spite of Bright, there was little reason to question Parliament's efficiency in foreign affairs as compared with other issues.

The later Victorian period saw a change of mood, as the left-wing Liberals became disenchanted with Gladstone's foreign policy. After the Radical tone of the 1880 'Midlothian' election campaign, Gladstone, returned to office, appeared to continue Tory policy by further extending the British Empire. Radical suspicion of foreign entanglements automatically implied their hostility to the annexation of Egypt. The pattern of European politics had also changed. Major nations had lined up into opposing groups: the Concert of Europe had been replaced by the concept of the balance of power. This produced a fear that Britain might become linked to one of the opposing camps and be engaged in war through prior commitments. Suspicion of all diplomacy was heightened by the knowledge that the Diplomatic Service remained an aristocratic preserve as the Foreign Office had been the one Department wholly to avoid Civil Service reforms. The growth of party organization and loyalty in the Commons strengthened the Cabinet and greatly increased the difficulty of reversing its policy by backbench action. Procedural restrictions on the rights of Members had been introduced in 1882 to contain obstruction by the Irish Nationalists. And the limited power of Parliament to control the content of treaties—in contrast to legislation—had been stressed by Bagehot.

These varied elements crystallised in a Commons' debate on March 19, 1886, on a backbench motion introduced by Henry Richard, Member for Merthyr Tydfil.[1] His motion read: 'That in the opinion of this House it is not just or expedient to embark in war, contract engagements involving grave responsibilities for the nation, and add territories to the Empire without the knowledge and consent of Parliament.' The debate was

[1] Richard was an unofficial leader of the Welsh non-conformist Members and was primarily interested in domestic issues, especially education. K. O. Morgan, *Wales in British Politics* (University of Wales, 1963), contains some material on Richard's influence and ideas. For the debate cf. Parl. Deb., 3rd series, Vol. 303, cols. 1386–1423.

unique as a largely abstract parliamentary discussion of the role of the legislature in foreign relations. Richard's speech was squarely in the Cobdenite tradition. He criticised the extension of Empire and the large number of foreign treaties that imposed military obligations upon us. While the Government could levy no tax whatever without parliamentary consent, an official acting in our name could plunge the nation into war. His distrust of diplomacy and diplomats was evident. Instead of being committed automatically to war under certain circumstances, the Commons should be able to propose conciliation through arbitration. To argue that the Commons controlled foreign policy through the power of the purse was illusory: if war started, inevitably it would carry on. The seconder of the motion, Rylands (Burnley) urged that the House should have the right to discuss treaties before ratification, and quoted the 1871 debate in the Lords on the Treaty of Washington when it was argued that as the Treaty had been negotiated by plenipotentiaries who 'engaged and promised upon the royal word', the Treaty must be upheld.[1] Speaking for the Opposition, Lord Randolph Churchill complained that the Radicals talked always in terms of principle and ignored realities: the motion would undermine existing agreements with foreign rulers which had been accepted by all parties. Prime Minister Gladstone defended the extent of executive power while accepting that 'it should be used with a full sense of what is due to the House and the Country.' The motion raised insuperable problems. International incidents that might lead to war occurred when the House was not sitting. Territorial annexation was a consequence of war and was sometimes difficult to avoid. It was rare for a Government to negotiate a treaty without some public knowledge of its policy, but an element of secrecy was essential. In the eighteenth century the Crown had sometimes communicated with Parliament on treaties about to be concluded but then there was no public reporting of Parliament: in 1886 the business of Parliament could not be kept confidential. Gladstone concluded by arguing that the motion was impractical since it attempted to bestow executive functions on the legislature.

The other remarkable feature of this occasion is that the

---

[1] Parl. Deb., 3rd series, Vol. 206, col. 1882.

motion was lost by a mere six votes,[1] 115 to 109. Including tellers, 75 Liberals and 36 Irish Nationalists supported the motion; 55 Liberals, 61 Conservatives and one Irish Independent voted against.[2] The low number of Members participating in the division was due to the day being Friday. Had a few more Conservatives absented themselves, the Government would have been caused some embarrassment.

Interest in the question of legislative control of foreign policy faded after the debate of March 1886 for a variety of reasons. Three months later came the historic vote on the Home Rule Bill which split the Liberal Party and kept it out of office for the greater part of the next twenty years. Thus Radical energies were used to attack Conservative Governments and perhaps were even more preoccupied with divisions in the Liberal Party on foreign policy.[3] Radical concern to improve the effectiveness of backbenchers was greater when their own nominal leaders were in power for in these conditions there was real hope of influencing policy. The existence of a Conservative administration called for different tactics—a public campaign of criticism which could be advanced by direct challenges within the existing pattern of parliamentary debates.

The 1886 motion had been drafted in broad and extreme terms.[4] Support was most widespread for the second of its propositions—that treaties should require parliamentary approval. This demand became orthodox Radical doctrine and was subsequently adopted by the Labour Party. The idea was not new in 1886. Fourteen years earlier Bagehot had argued strongly in its favour in the introduction to the second edition of his *English Constitution*. Bagehot put and countered three arguments against the submission of treaties to Parliament. It might

[1] For comment on the parliamentary situation in March 1886, see S. Maccoby *English Radicalism 1886–1914* (Allen Unwin, 1953), p. 19.

[2] I am grateful to Mrs Anne Harris for this analysis.

[3] These have been extensively analysed by R. H. Gross, *Factors and Variations in Liberal and Radical Opinion on Foreign Policy, 1885–1899*, a D. Phil. thesis in the Bodleian.

[4] It secured what may be termed the late-Utilitarian approval of Henry Sidgwick, in spite of his admission that the peculiar difficulties of foreign relations must limit the effectiveness of a legislature and necessitated in this field a greater degree of trust in the actions of Ministers and officials: *Elements of Politics* (Macmillan, 1891), pp. 438–40.

sometimes be inappropriate 'for Ministers to state clearly the motives which induced them to agree to foreign compacts.' To this Bagehot replied that history showed that the reticence of diplomacy had done more harm than good—a theme that will be repeated in the following pages. The second objection, that Parliament was not always in session, he met by arguing that few treaties were urgent and that Parliament could be re-assembled if the need were sufficient. The third problem was that submission of treaties for parliamentary approval would strengthen the power of the House of Lords: this Bagehot felt could be risked without fear of serious difficulty, for the Lords must defer to the will of the Commons and the country even where their own judgment might guide them otherwise.

When the Liberals were returned to office in 1906 their leaders, in spite of pressure, maintained the refusal of earlier Governments to make treaties available for discussion prior to ratification.[1] However, the Agadir crisis and the revelation in 1911 of the secret Anglo-French agreements of 1904 intensified concern among Liberal Members over the conduct of foreign policy. Seventy of them formed a backbench Foreign Affairs Group—a short-lived forerunner of the unofficial party committees now firmly established. The Group were concerned with secret diplomacy, the influence of professional diplomats and tended to be pro-German rather than pro-French in outlook.[2] Outside Parliament a Foreign Policy Committee was formed under the presidency of the veteran Lord Courtney. Its aims included the advocacy of 'greater publicity as to foreign affairs and fuller Parliamentary control of the main lines of policy and of all important agreements concluded with other Governments'.[3] One result of this activity was the publication of an official return showing how international agreements were treated by Parliaments of other countries.[4]

[1] H. C. Deb., Vol. 5, col. 1399.
[2] T. P. Conwell-Evans, *Foreign Policy from a Back-Bench*, (O.U.P., 1932), pp. 80–4.
[3] G. P. Gooch, *Life of Lord Courtney*, (Macmillan, 1920), pp. 572–3. A threepenny pamphlet set out the arguments with admirable clarity: A. Ponsonby, *Democracy and the Control of Foreign Affairs*, (Fifield, 1913).
[4] 1912–13, Cd. 6102, xviii. This was initiated by a request from the Commons: H. C. Deb., Vol. 31, col. 673. A revised up-to-date version was issued in 1924: Cmd 2285, 1924–5, xxiii. These documents are based on

The outbreak of war in 1914 provided both a check and a stimulus to Radical critics. Administrative requirements and the social atmosphere engendered by a war-time situation weakened claims for fuller activity by Parliament. Yet concern at the seemingly accidental way the conflict started and at the horrors of war, combined with a conviction that affairs should be better conducted in the post-war era, produced a fresh element in the political climate. A new popular movement, the Union of Democratic Control, was born in September, 1914, and steadily gathered momentum throughout the war. It was a unique example of a mass organisation being concerned with the *method* of conducting foreign affairs. It had three main objects. To secure real parliamentary control over foreign policy and prevent it being shaped in secret and forced upon the country as an established fact. When peace returned to communicate with democratic parties in other countries in order to create international understanding based on popular parties. To prevent a peace settlement of a type that would provide a basis for future antagonism and war.[1] It was not a 'stop-the-war' movement; rather it held that war might have been prevented had the public known of the Government's commitments. Its complaint against the Government centred on Grey's statement on August 3, 1914, that if the German fleet came through the channel to undertake operations against France, the British fleet would give France all the protection in its power. This pledge was the consequence of an understanding between French and British military and naval experts in 1911 which led to the French fleet being in the Mediterranean leaving their channel coast unprotected. The UDC argued that this 'understanding' was contrary to earlier undertakings by the Prime Minister and Foreign Secretary that no secret arrangements existed between Britain and a European Power that would force us to take part in a future European war.[2] Since Britain's entry to the war had been forced by the German invasion of Belgium, not the presence of the German reports from our ambassadors in the countries concerned. Essentially they are formal expositions of constitutional procedures; nevertheless, they demonstrate that by 1924 it was fairly general practice for legislatures to have a special committee dealing with international questions.

Why have no subsequent editions of this document been produced?

[1] H. M. Swanwick, *Builders of Peace*, (Swarthmore Press, 1924), p.32.
[2] H. C. Deb., Vol. 50, col. 1317 and Vol. 53, col. 456.

24

fleet in the Channel, the UDC case lost some of its force. However, it could still urge with cogency, on those willing to listen in the jingoist war-time atmosphere, that such secret unofficial obligations should not be permitted again.

The UDC did urge 'peace by negotiation' but was not pacifist, although many of its supporters were pacifists. It had to suffer abuse in the popular press that commonly described the organization as pro-German. Its meetings were broken up by rowdy hostile elements. But the Union flourished, local branches were established throughout the country and by 1918 many trade union organizations representing 650,000 members had affiliated to it. Prominent amongst the earliest supporters were two Liberal M.P.s Charles Trevelyan[1] and Arthur Ponsonby and two Labour M.P.s Ramsay MacDonald and Fred Jowett. Other notable supporters were Norman Angell, Bertrand Russell, H. N. Brailsford and E. D. Morel who became the secretary and driving force of the organization.

The UDC was almost unique among left-wing movements of protest in that it never split and did not suffer dramatic resignations. Certainly its leading members were not always in agreement. There were differences over the value of international institutions to prevent war. Some argued that a league of nations would help to check secret diplomacy: others claimed that as the causes of war were economic, war could not be prevented merely by the establishment of fresh institutions operating within the framework of the capitalist system. It held together perhaps, because it made no attempt to act as a political party, but only to serve as an educational medium, with a broad message that pre-war governments had mishandled foreign affairs in conditions of secrecy, that matters must be better managed in future, and that the best guarantee of progress was widespread public understanding of foreign policy problems both in this country and abroad.

The fullest account of the pattern of ideas propagated by the UDC is to be found in a book by Arthur Ponsonby, *Democracy*

[1] Trevelyan, then Parliamentary Secretary to the Board of Education, resigned from the Asquith Government at the outbreak of war. So did Morley, Secretary of State for India, and John Burns, President of the Local Government Board, both of whom retired from public life. Trevelyan and Ponsonby subsequently joined the Labour Party.

and Diplomacy.[1] He argued that as diplomacy had failed to produce peace and security, foreign policy should be determined by public opinion. It was true that no machinery existed in some countries to discover public attitudes; in Britain such machinery did exist but was not used effectively in connection with foreign affairs, partly because of secrecy, partly because of an unspoken agreement between leaders of the Government and Opposition to avoid debate. Ponsonby accepted that popular opinion was not necessarily pacific or correct—but if it were acted on by the Government and proved wrong—then at least people would suffer for their own mistakes. To those who argued that militaristic sentiment was easily aroused among the masses, Ponsonby replied that this was due to the limited and biased information made available by the Press and to a mode of thought encouraged by national leaders. An informed public would not be misled or scared. The case for popular control of foreign policy was essentially the case for democracy; there was no basic difference between domestic issues and international questions. The need for confidential dealings with foreign governments was over-stressed by diplomats for purposes of self-preservation. Owing to widespread ignorance the Government tended to discount public opinion on foreign affairs, but the Government itself was largely responsible for this lack of knowledge. Standards of international behaviour would improve if the public had more influence because the standards of morality between states were significantly lower than the standards which governed the general pattern of behaviour between individuals.

Ponsonby did not argue that all international negotiations should be public, but merely that the broad lines of Government policy should be known so that they could be judged. Parliament was the only forum in which opinions could be expressed effectively. It was vital, both as a channel of communication and as a safety valve. Open action by Ministers in constant touch with Parliament would strengthen the British position as other states would recognize that the British Foreign Secretary had added authority derived from popular support. But Parliament could not perform its duty competently unless it were fully informed. Ponsonby's book also reflected Radical suspicion of

[1] Methuen, 1915.

the Foreign Office and Diplomatic Service which had been heightened by the resistance of the Foreign Office to the Civil Service reforms of 1855 and 1870.[1] He advocated specific changes in parliamentary procedure, regular reports by the Foreign Secretary to Parliament, discussion of foreign policy by a special committee, and the need for Parliamentary consent to the declaration of war, international treaties and any other foreign commitment in order to prevent confidential understandings and obligations of honour.

The crusade against secret diplomacy was greatly aided in 1917–18 by two events, the Russian revolution and the entry of the United States into the war. The new regime in Moscow, bent on demonstrating its utter rejection of the doings of the Czarist government, published a number of secret treaties made by the Allied Powers. These were designed to redefine territorial boundaries in the post-war period and encouraged Italy and Roumania to join the Allies through the promise of annexations when peace was made. The secret treaties were printed in the Russian Press and were partly reproduced in the *Manchester Guardian*, and other British newspapers: subsequently they were issued, together with maps and commentary, in a book by Seymour Cocks.[2] Besides the treaties with Italy and Roumania, there was an agreement between Britain, France and Russia to partition Turkish lands in Asia, a treaty between Russia and Japan and a Franco-Russian agreement on the reduction of Germany, which included pushing Germany's western frontier back to the Rhine. Since the Allies had agreed to make peace in common this arrangement involved Britain. The Lloyd George Cabinet were disturbed by the idea of the frontier at the Rhine: ultimately Balfour told the Commons that we had never expressed approval of it.[3]

A wholly new influence on future peacemaking emerged when the United States entered the war. President Wilson had no prior commitments in Europe and distrusted the patterns of diplomacy which had led to the war. His 'fourteen points' opened with the demand for 'open covenants of peace, openly

---

[1] Peter G. Richards, *Patronage in British Government* (London: Allen Unwin, Toronto: University of Toronto Press, 1963), p. 55.

[2] *The Secret Treaties* (Union of Democratic Control, n.d.).

[3] H. C. Deb., Vol. 100, col. 2017.

arrived at'. Lloyd George indicated his broad support for Wilson's policy. This served to please the powerful new ally; it pleased Radical and Labour opinion in this country; it reflected also the embarrassment felt by the British Government at the publication of the secret treaties, further aggravated by the disagreement with France over the Rhine frontier. In 1918 the Union of Democratic Control could feel that it had achieved a large measure of success and its reputation was certainly enhanced. But the success had come not from its own efforts but through the coincidence of major events in distant places.

The Treaty of Versailles and the negotiations that preceeded it brought widespread disillusion. This was intensified by the manifest failure to adhere to Wilson's principle of 'open covenants of peace, openly arrived at', for much of the vital negotiation at Versailles was conducted in private between Britain, France and the United States, with both their minor allies and defeated enemies excluded from the discussion.[1] Originally, of course, Wilson had been too idealistic. Ponsonby, with a greater sense of reality, had never argued that detailed negotiation should be undertaken in the full glare of publicity; he appreciated that negotiation requires give-and-take, compromise and bargaining, which need an element of privacy. His concern, as shown above, was that principles of foreign policy should be widely understood and that the end-product of negotiations, treaties, should be subject to freely expressed approval by Parliament. Wilson, however, succeeded in creating confusion in the public mind between 'open diplomacy' and the 'popular control of diplomacy'; the distinction between policy and administration is never readily understood.[2]

The attention of the Union of Democratic Control turned away from the constitutional problem of how foreign policy should be controlled, to immediate policy issues of the time. Its main concern became the severity of the peace terms, which it foretold contained the cause of future war. A feeling grew that the battle for greater democratic influence in foreign affairs had, in large part, been successfully completed. With the emergence of Soviet Russia, and the United States, European aristocracy no

[1] This was due in part to the difficulties created by the secret treaties. H. Nicolson, *Peacemaking 1919* (Constable, 1933), Book 1, Chs. VI, VII.
[2] H. Nicolson, *Diplomacy* (O.U.P., 3rd edn. 1963), p. 84.

longer dominated the diplomatic scene. In Britain, Labour became the official Opposition: after 1922 supporters of the UDC were always on a front-bench in the Commons, usually in opposition but occasionally in office. Parliamentary discussion of foreign affairs was, therefore, more vigorous than before 1914. The existence of the League of Nations provided a new international forum for the discussion of international questions. Article 18 of the Covenant of the League promised to bring an end to secret pacts; it read 'Every treaty or international engagement entered into hereafter by any Member of the League shall be forthwith registered with the Secretariat and shall as soon as possible be published by it. No such treaty or international engagement shall be binding until so registered'. Until disenchantment with the League developed in the nineteen-thirties, this type of provision was regarded as a valuable safeguard. Progress was made even on the question of the power of the British Parliament to scrutinize treaties. The rejection by the United States' Senate of the Treaty of Versailles provided dramatic demonstration that a democratic legislature could control foreign policy. Strong pressure developed in the Commons for the right to consider treaties prior to ratification. Then in 1923 a convention to regulate the status of Tangier was circulated to the Press, but not to Members. The Foreign Office spokesman agreed that there was no reason to withhold it from Members: he added 'I think it is becoming more and more a custom not to ratify Treaties without giving the House of Commons the opportunity suggested' (i.e. of discussion).[1] With the advent of the Labour Government in 1924 the right of Parliament to review treaties prior to ratification was formalised in the Ponsonby rule—named after Arthur Ponsonby then Under-Secretary at the Foreign Office.[2]

Thus in the early nineteen-twenties the ideas of the Union of Democratic Control were triumphant.[3] They received broad support from Viscount Bryce who suggested that while the means of implementation of foreign policy must be decided by

[1] H. C. Deb., Vol. 169, col. 138.
[2] For developments after 1924 see pp. 43–5.
[3] This organization was wound up in 1966. For many years before that it had been but a shadow of its former self, occasionally issuing pamphlets expressing a Left-wing viewpoint.

Ministers, the ends to be pursued could well be determined in consultation with the populace. Ignorance was not so widespread as to prevent effective popular decision-making on the major issues of policy. Working class opinion had been in conflict with that of Ministers over the American civil war, the Russo-Turkish conflict and the Boer War, and Bryce argued that these cases showed that popular judgement was usually right. It was at least as likely to be right on the ends of foreign policy as monarchs or oligarchs whose mistakes had been 'less pardonable and more harmful to the peace and progress of nations'.[1] Since relations between individuals were conducted on a higher moral plane than relations between states, it was helpful to bring personal standards of morality into international disputes.[2] This, of course, is development of the liberal belief that judgements should and would be based on conscience rather than interests.

Such optimism became unfashionable in Britain in the nineteen-thirties.[3] Democracy was attacked because it was based on discussion and compromise and so was weak and timid in defending national interests. These doubts were not new: it was noted above how de Tocqueville had questioned the competence of democracy in foreign affairs. Contemporary events powerfully reinforced this trend of thought, notably the successes of dictatorships in Germany, Italy and Spain. These contrasted harshly with the hesitations of Britain and France and the Peace Ballot of 1935 when eleven million people in this country subscribed to the principles of disarmament and resistance to aggression by collective security, principles which were, in the circumstances, utopian if not contradictory. Among Left-wing thinkers zeal for traditional parliamentary democracy was diminished by the prospect of achievements in the Soviet Union. A broad consensus of views developed which equated

[1] *Modern Democracies* (Macmillan, 1921), Vol. II, p. 420.

[2] Cf. Viscount Bryce: *International Relations* (Macmillan 1922), Lecture VI.

[3] In the United States the cause of what may be termed primitive or market place democracy remained powerful at this period. The Ludlow Amendment to the Constitution which required a national referendum to confirm a congressional declaration of war—save in the case of invasion—was defeated in 1937 by the House of Representatives only by the narrow margin of 209 votes to 188.

democracy with incompetence and ineffectiveness, especially in the spheres of defence and foreign affairs.[1]

Naturally the successful British resistance to Nazi aggression, especially the determination shown in 1940, produced a new outlook. A. D. Lindsay in *The Modern Democratic State*[2] argued that the public must be consulted because they alone could know 'where the shoe pinches' or how they were affected by state action. In foreign affairs the case was different since the subject was remote from ordinary experience, but the people must still be consulted because otherwise, Lindsay urged, political leaders cannot know how much support they will receive in time of crisis. This was a slightly more complex way of expressing the wartime belief that free men fought better than those serving dictators. But Lindsay's book contains a curious bundle of arguments. The idea that the public at large want to live their own lives and do not understand how foreign policy may affect them was a throwback to the nineteen thirties. When Lindsay published this work and, indeed, ever since, it has been abundantly clear to the majority of voters that their well-being and their very existence depends far more upon international developments than on domestic political issues. Certainly, international affairs attract less public attention than their importance demands, but this is partly because the measure of agreement on basic issues between party leaders has stultified argument and is partly due to a sense of powerlessness that tends to deaden response. Further, Linday's argument for democratic foreign policy is limited to situations in which there is a threat of war and when the nation needs aid from each individual: fortunately not all foreign issues involve a real possibility of war. And to use Dahl's terminology, Lindsay is putting forward a maximization theory, not an ethical theory; he does not claim that a state is better if people are consulted, merely that it is stronger as they will then do more to support their leaders. But what if leaders by demagogy and skilful propaganda put up a successful show of consultation which produced equally good results? Were this

[1] A full discussion of these issues would involve an examination of the history of anti-democratic theory. On the incompetence of democracy see D. Spitz: *Patterns of Anti-Democratic Thought* (Macmillan, New York, 1949), Ch. 4.
[2] (O.U.P., 1943), pp. 269–76.

shown to be possible, Lindsay's case for democratic influence on the conduct of international affairs disintegrates.

PUBLIC OPINION AND FOREIGN POLICY

The fear that popular control of foreign policy implies that ultimate authority will be surrendered immediately to uninformed public clamour is wholly misconceived. Democracy in Britain—and elsewhere—does not work in this way. Discussion of public policy takes place on an hierarchical basis. The vital arguments over foreign policy are conducted by a limited and knowledgeable élite, centred on Whitehall, Westminster, Fleet Street and some London clubs. Through the mass media some politicians and publicists then perform the arguments in front of the general public. Not everyone is attentive and the amount of interest varies. For foreign affairs the interest level is normally lower than that for domestic issues. A National Opinion Poll survey made just before the 1964 General Election showed that 10% of the respondents thought that foreign policy would be particularly important to them in the election: the three subjects most frequently mentioned as important were the cost of living 72%, education 29% and housing 27%. At moments of major international crisis the balance of interest is reversed. The more attentive members of the public tend to be among the better informed and they fill the role of opinion-leaders in workplaces, clubs, local trade union branches, local political party meetings and other centres of political discussion. Thus a continuous public debate is conducted of fluctuating intensity and various levels of quality. When discussion flares into strong controversy, public demonstrations occur, organised and supported by the younger and most vigorous advocates of the more extreme policies. This public discussion ultimately has an influence on those in the seats of authority who make decisions: to use the new popular but inelegant jargon—there is a 'feedback' process working through many channels which conveys and crystallises public reactions. An important channel is the individual Member of Parliament who is influenced both by the debate amongst other members of the national élite and by his constituents' reaction to it, especially that of the leading members of his constituency association who form a local élite. Another indicator of opinion is the resolutions from local

branches submitted to national party and trade union gatherings. Opinion poll enquiries test the mood of the general
public.

The impact of the feedback is sluggish and erratic. Ministers
do not change a major policy merely because an opinion poll
demonstrates its unpopularity, although they may be encouraged to adhere to a policy which a poll shows to have wide support.
It will be shown below in Chapter VII that resolutions at party
conferences do not easily change national policy. Members of
Parliament are also well insulated from pressures of opinion, so
long as they remain true to the policy of their own party, by the
rigidity of our party system. Their independence of 'instructions'
from constituencies was stressed by Burke in his famous speech
to the electors of Bristol. 'Your representative owes you, not
his industry only, but his judgment; and he betrays, instead of
serving you, if he sacrifices it to your opinion'. This doctrine is
accepted gratefully by Members as a statement of constitutional
orthodoxy. Of course, public opinion is potent at the moment of
a general election, but if the major political parties are in basic
agreement on foreign policy, the force of the feedback on these
issues will be blunted.

Popular control of foreign policy cannot mean that decisions
are made by the counting of heads. Yet it does require that
three conditions be satisfied.[1] First, the argument among the
knowledgeable élite must be free, unfettered and not deprived of
vital information by state censorship. Beyond this élite there
are many levels of political awareness: as one descends the
hierarchy, the numbers participating increase and information
and influence decline. Second, the mass audience must be able
to attend to the debate on policy and participate in it. Third, the
political system must ensure that those who exercise authority
are sensitive to the reactions of the mass audience—this implies
periodic elections and an organised opposition able to criticise
Government actions.

The two central elements of the Radical dissatisfaction described in the first part of this chapter were stimulated by a
desire that these conditions should become more fully effective.
The lack of information, challenged by Bright, led to criticism

[1] For a slightly different formulation of these conditions see Gabriel
Almond, *The American People and Foreign Policy* (Praeger, 1960), p. 139.

of secret diplomacy and the feeling in the Union of Democratic Control that Ministers had misled Parliament before the outbreak of war in 1914. Exactly the same suspicions were aroused by the Suez crisis of 1956. The other source of contention was that Ministers were insufficiently exposed to opinion in Parliament and elsewhere. In consequence, there arose demands for institutional change—that Parliament should be required to approve the ratification of treaties and that the Commons should have a committee specialising in foreign affairs. The Union of Democratic Control having aroused more interest in foreign policy was then in a stronger position to insist that the 'feedback' channels for public opinion should be strengthened.

Through the mass media there are now fuller facilities than ever before to enable the public to listen to the central arguments over public policy. The facilities are there, but how far are they used? It is widely agreed that the electorate are more concerned with domestic issues than international questions and this may well affect how Members balance the distribution of their time between subjects. Save in a major international crisis the main sources of political argument are economic advantage and issues involving equality: in the public mind these seem to be far removed from the business of the Foreign Office. Specialist opinion sees the position quite differently. British entry into Europe would provoke highly complex estimates of economic advantage. Left-wing opinion views the struggle in Vietnam at least partly as an issue involving equality. But in both cases the arguments are sophisticated and leave the mass audience unexcited. Rhodesia attracts wider attention because the principle of equality has an obvious application and, for some people, family and economic connexions stimulate concern.

How far the public are less well informed on foreign affairs cannot be precisely measured. The Gallup Poll commonly shows a higher 'Don't Know' response on international topics than other issues. Yet the significance of this difference could be over-estimated: it is possible that people are more willing to admit ignorance, or say they have no opinion on a foreign issue, whereas on a domestic issue pride may demand that a positive answer be given to the pollster. When the mass public are seriously muddled then the politicians are to blame for confusing public discussion. The factual argument over Britain's defences at the 1964 General Election was clearly responsible for the perplexity revealed in the Gallup Poll report in February, 1965, which showed that 30% of those questioned thought that Britain had an independent nuclear deterrent, 29% thought we had not while the remaining 41% answered 'Don't Know'. This result was quite untypical because it concerned a matter of fact rather than opinion. There is no consensus on other international issues, notably the wisdom of American policy in Vietnam, but this is a division of opinion, not simply confusion about the realities of a situation. Yet it is quite certain that the mass of people cannot be well informed about the aspirations, difficulties and strength of purpose of foreign governments. For the democrat this does nothing to weaken the case for popular influence over foreign policy: he must argue that the right of the public to be consulted applies over the whole range of government policy. The public can be concerned only with broad principles; even their elected representatives in the Commons can rarely be concerned with the details of international negotiation. But any Minister who ignores evidence of a movement of popular opinion, out of contempt for public ignorance, is guilty of overwhelming arrogance. Certainly, information should assist judgement. It remains true that recent British history is littered with examples of how our statesmen, presumably briefed with all the resources of their Departments, were still able to be utterly wrong about the intentions and reactions of foreign governments.

The case for full parliamentary scrutiny of foreign policy is that in a democratic society Government leaders must be accountable for their actions to elected representatives of the whole community and that they should be forced to reconsider their policies in the light of public debate. The following chapters consider the hindrances to this process.

CHAPTER III

The Royal Prerogative

TRADITIONALLY the British Monarch has played a leading role in the conduct of our foreign relations. An absolute Monarch with unchallenged power could determine, perhaps by personal whim, the pattern of our overseas alliances. Even as the Cabinet developed and its authority grew, or as the House of Commons achieved a dominant position in the state, the king (or queen) continued to be actively concerned with foreign affairs. One reason for this was inter-marriage among the royal families of Europe. More significant was the fact that diplomatic protocol demanded in various ways that the Head of State must be associated with relationships with foreign powers. Queen Victoria's strong views on foreign affairs not infrequently brought her into conflict with her Ministers. Today, although the personal influence of the Monarch has waned, our past history is still important in that the basis of our association with other states depends in large part upon the Royal Prerogative.

The classic definition of the Royal Prerogative is that of Dicey, 'the residue of discretionary or arbitrary authority which at any time is legally left in the hands of the Crown'. In the field of foreign affairs, the Prerogative covers the right to make war or peace, to make treaties, to recognise foreign states or their Governments, to appoint diplomatic representatives abroad and to receive representatives of other states. Thus the Monarch is still personally concerned with the ratification of treaties and the reception of ambassadors. Royal trips oversea and the entertainment of visiting Heads of State at Buckingham Palace help to strengthen friendly relations with other countries. But the powers of the Royal Prerogative are exercised by Ministers who hold their positions by virtue of the support of a majority in the House of Commons. This led Dicey to argue that the Royal Prerogative greatly strengthened the democratic character of our system of government. 'The survival of the prerogative, conferring as it does wide discretionary authority upon the Cabinet, . . . immensely increases the authority of the House of Commons and ultimately of the constituencies by which that House is returned.'[1] Dicey argued further that whereas the Lords could destroy Government legislation, the Lords could not—but the Commons could—destroy a Government whose use of Prerogative powers was objectionable. Clearly, there was greater validity for this view when *The Law and the Constitution* was published in 1885 than there is in modern conditions. Even so, it remains true that the Prerogative powers are used broadly in accordance with popular will. Equally, since the House of Commons is restrained by strong party discipline, it is well understood abroad that in normal circumstances British Ministers can negotiate secure in the knowledge that their actions will obtain parliamentary approval.

In some fields the existence of the Royal Prerogative has the effect of limiting parliamentary discussion. Parliamentary questions are barred on the prerogative of mercy, ecclesiastical patronage and on the award of individual honours; this prohibition does not extend to foreign affairs. Indeed, one purpose of this chapter is to demonstrate that the Prerogative imposes no artificial limitations on parliamentary discussion of the issues of foreign policy. It is also concerned to show how far Parliament is associated with major decisions in this field, questions of war, treaty-making and diplomatic recognition. Discussion of how far present arrangements are adequate and satisfactory will be the subject of later chapters.

THE DECLARATION OF WAR[2]

The formalities of a declaration of war may be completed in at least two ways. In 1914 a Royal Proclamation was issued on the authority of an Order-in-Council. In 1939 there was no Royal Proclamation but the *London Gazette* published a notification of a state of war with Germany that had been issued from the Privy Council Office. Thus the declaration is an executive act

---

[1] *The Law and the Constitution*, 9th ed. edited by E. C. S. Wade (Macmillan 1939), p. 466.

[2] For a valuable but out-of-date discussion see F. R. Flournoy, *Parliament and War* (King, 1927).

and no consent by Parliament is needed. There is no requirement that the elected legislature shall assent to the most far-reaching of all decisions that a government may be called upon to make. Minor bills may consume hours of parliamentary time: the determination to start a major war could, in theory, go undiscussed at least until irrevocable action had been taken. This is a bleak picture of the efficacy of our democracy and may be contrasted unfavourably to the position in the United States where only the Congress can declare war. Further, and this is inevitably the case in the United States as well as all democratic countries, the executive has control over the disposition of its armed forces and can use its influence to aggravate the diplomatic situation. In other words, a Government can, if it so chooses, make war inevitable. So even if the House of Commons had the right to give prior approval to the start of hostilities, this would not enable it to control every situation, especially when another state had been provoked into attacking British territory.

Is discussion about the formal rights of Parliament in this matter wholly unrealistic? Parliament does, in fact, debate any international crisis that develops. When an emergency occurs in a recess, Parliament can be hastily summoned should British interests be deeply involved; if a severe crisis were to develop during a general election campaign when Parliament was dissolved, it would be impossible to consult the elected representatives of the people. Leaving this difficulty aside, it is the basic feature of the British Constitution that Ministers are a part of our Parliament and depend on the support of the House of Commons, and it is highly unlikely in the field of foreign affairs that a major gap could develop between the views of the Cabinet and majority opinion in the Commons. Another reason for being unconcerned about the rights of Parliament is that Parliament has very limited influence in the nuclear age. If the major nuclear powers, the United States and the Soviet Union, come to the brink of war, what can the British Parliament do to ease the situation? Harsh reality demands that the answer would almost certainly be 'Nothing'. It is not merely military powerlessness that renders Parliament impotent: the time-scale in a crisis may be too short for opinions expressed in parliamentary debate to have any influence. In these circumstances any argument about whether Parliament should insist on giving prior approval to a war becomes farcical. Yet it is still the case that not every situation that may lead to hostilities involves a confrontation between major nuclear powers. Suez is one example. There is always a great danger of escalation, but when the chance of immediate wholesale conflagration is less, the influence of Parliament could be more important. So the convention that Parliament discusses international affairs at moments of tension is still of major significance.

To revert to constitutional discussion, it can be argued that a Government cannot start hostilities without parliamentary approval because it may not incur expenditure on purposes other than those covered by the estimates that have to receive parliamentary sanction—a view held strongly by Gladstone.[1] But this doctrine cannot cover a situation in which British territory is attacked, nor could it prevent a war-minded Government from undertaking provocative diplomatic actions. Gladstone's theory has an attractive nineteenth-century flavour, but it has no great value as a safeguard of parliamentary rights. The ultimate check on a Cabinet is, of course, the right of Parliament to refuse to vote money to support its policies. But once a war has started, the situation progressively becomes less easy for a parliament to control. On one occasion the Commons has refused to support a war. In 1856 the Palmerston Government opened hostilities in China without parliamentary approval and subsequently this policy was rejected in the Commons by a majority of sixteen votes. Thereupon Palmerston dissolved Parliament and obtained a majority at the following election. Today such a situation is unlikely to occur: it could apply only in the case of a remote, small-scale conflict and in a parliamentary situation of greatly weakened party discipline.

The pattern of parliamentary activity when faced with an immediate prospect of war can best be shown by reference to events in 1914 and 1939. At the start of the European crisis in 1914 opinion was confused, the Cabinet was divided and there was both pro-German and anti-war feeling in Parliament. Probably because of the uncertainty a debate on the international situation was avoided until August 3rd—the eve of war—when

[1] D. G. Bishop, *The Administration of British Foreign Relations* (Syracuse University Press, 1961), p. 10.

the Commons spent the whole day discussing the crisis.[1] Grey, the Foreign Secretary, presented an unemotional, restrained report; he stressed that the Government had entered into no binding commitments with France, apart from an undertaking to protect its Channel coast from the German Fleet, and discussed the German ultimatum to Belgium and the appeal from Belgium for our support. The problem of how Britain should act was presented to the House as one of honour and moral obligation. He was followed by Conservative and Irish spokesmen who supported Government policy and by Ramsay MacDonald who opposed it. After an adjournment the debate was continued by backbenchers. No vote was taken, but it was clear that the Government enjoyed the support of an overwhelming majority in the Commons; their opponents had many opportunities to test the feeling of the House by challenging a division on any of the emergency legislation made necessary by the state of war—but they did not do so. In 1939 there was greater parliamentary discussion prior to the declaration of war on Germany. On August 24th the Commons was summoned to review the threatening international scene, and it passed the Emergency Powers (Defence) Bill. There was another debate on August 29th and daily meetings from September 1st, so there were four debates before the nation engaged in war. At no stage did the Commons pass a formal resolution in favour of war with Germany but it was even more certain than in 1914 that the House supported the Cabinet. A few divisions were forced on the emergency legislation but the number of Members opposing the measures was always below ten. Both in 1914 and 1939 the mood of the Commons was rather more aggressive than that of the Cabinet; indeed, in 1914 three Ministers, Burns, Morley and Trevelyan, resigned as they would not support the war policy.

These precedents provide persuasive evidence that a Government does not use the prerogative power to go to war unless it has the support of the Commons. Unfortunately, this proposition has more recently been damaged by the Suez incident which is discussed in Chapter IX. But the Suez case does show that if a Government engages in hostilities without a solid base of parliamentary support, then the chances of a successful outcome of its policy are substantially reduced.

[1] H. C. Deb., Vol. 65, cols. 1809–84.

TREATIES

The task of treaty negotiation with foreign powers is essentially a part of the functions of the executive. Some treaties contain a clause which stipulates that the treaty will come into effect only when ratified by the parties thereto. The process of ratification is again an executive act which consists of fixing the Great Seal to a copy of the treaty and the exchange of documents certifying ratification with the other governments concerned. Ratification is normally automatic once a treaty has been signed, for the signature involves a moral commitment by the Government of the day. However, there have been two exceptions to the normal pattern of events during this century. In 1909 the Declaration of London was approved by the Commons but rejected by the Lords and, in consequence, was never ratified by the King. In 1924 the minority Labour Government of Ramsay MacDonald concluded trade and debt agreements with Russia but these had not been considered by Parliament before its dissolution: Labour were defeated at the subsequent election and the new Conservative administration decided not to ratify the treaty.

Many negotiations with foreign powers result in arrangements less formal than a treaty. Indeed in the 1963 Index to the Treaty Series of White Papers (Cmnd. 2336) only one of the ninety-three documents listed is officially described as a treaty. The more usual designations are 'Agreement', 'Exchange of Notes' or 'Convention'. There is some flexibility in this matter for international law prescribes neither the form nor the procedures for the making of treaties. Our own law and practice, in contrast with that of some other states, is equally silent on treaty-making procedure. Thus the terminology chosen is purely a matter of convenience and most frequently denotes a greater or lesser degree of formality. In the following pages the word 'treaty' will be used loosely to denote any diplomatic arrangement with another country. But it must be stressed that there is no necessary connection between the importance of a treaty and the amount of preparation and formality which accompanied it. Major decisions are sometimes made in hasty face-to-face negotiations between powerful politicians—for example, the Agreements of Munich, Yalta and Nassau.

The extent to which Parliament is called upon to approve treaties is partly a legal matter and partly a political problem. From a strictly legal viewpoint it seems that there are four categories of treaty that demand parliamentary assent. Some treaties cannot be made effective without some alteration to our existing law[1] or may impose actually or contingently a financial obligation on the British taxpayer: such treaties are not ratified until the necessary legislation has been either passed or accepted in principle by Parliament. Second, a treaty which attempts to increase the rights of the Crown will not be enforced by the courts without legislation.[2] The third category covers any treaty which itself demands the express consent of Parliament. Finally, it is customary for treaties involving the cession of territory to receive statutory confirmation for territorial changes inevitably affect the rights of some British subjects. When a colony attains independence its new status is sanctioned by an Act of Parliament which formally confers independence, makes adjustments in the law of nationality and perhaps defines the area of the colony. Whether the Crown has the right under the Royal Prerogative to cede territory without parliamentary consent is a matter of legal argument. Holdsworth was of the opinion that it has such power.[3] But since the cession of Heligoland to Germany in 1890 there have been many cases in which treaties involving territorial transfer have been approved by Parliament in subsequent legislation.[4] It is thus regular practice, if not a binding constitutional convention, for legislative sanction to be obtained.

Apart from the types of treaty listed above, there is no legal requirement for any parliamentary consultation. Whether parliamentary discussion takes place is wholly a political question. But there would be no point in attempting to hide a

---

[1] Ratification of international conventions concerned with industrial matters and labour conditions fall within this category. In such cases it is customary for the Government to have full prior consultations with interested organisations. Cf. the case-study by Gerald Rhodes on international standards of accommodation for merchant seamen: *Administrators in Action*, Vol. II (Allen & Unwin, 1965).

[2] *The Zamora* (1916) 2 A.C.77: *The Parliament Belge* (1879) 4 P.D. 129.

[3] *Law Quarterly Review* (1942), Vol. 58, p. 179.

[4] The examples are given by Lord McNair, *Law of Treaties* (O.U.P., 1961), p. 96.

treaty away in order to avoid controversy for if the Opposition objects strongly to any treaty (or agreement) a debate on it could always be forced by tabling a Vote of Censure. One of the best known facts of our constitutional history is that in 1712 the Tory administration had to use the Royal Prerogative to create a dozen new peers to overcome Whig opposition in the Lords to the Treaty of Utrecht. Parliamentary scrutiny can be avoided only if a Government enters into secret engagements. In the early years of this century there was much concern and controversy over secret diplomacy. Sir Edward Grey, Foreign Secretary 1905–16, was firmly opposed to the creation of secret obligations,[1] but the preceding Governments had made a number of unpublished agreements. Chief among these was the Anglo-French agreement of 1904 (made public in 1911) designed to strengthen the position of France in Morocco and that of Britain in Egypt. This incident, combined with distaste for much of the covert negotiation that was known to have taken place during the First World War, produced the demand that parliamentary assent to treaties should always be obtained, a demand stimulated by the Union of Democratic Control. The rejection of the Treaty of Versailles by the United States Senate demonstrated that legislative approval of treaties could be a vital political decision and not an automatic acceptance of executive action.

The Labour Government of 1924 accepted the case for parliamentary supervision of international agreements. 'During our term of office we shall inform the House of all agreements, commitments and understandings which in any way bind the nation to specific action in certain circumstances.'[2] Important treaties would be submitted automatically to the Commons: other agreements would be discussed if the demand arose. All treaties were to lay on the table of the House for twenty-one days prior to ratification. These arrangements constituted the so-called Ponsonby Rule.[3] Naturally, the Labour Government

---

[1] G. M. Trevelyan, *Grey of Fallodon* (Longmans, 1937), pp. 124, 240.
[2] H. C. Deb., Vol. 171, col. 2005.
[3] Arthur Ponsonby, then Under-Secretary of State at the Foreign Office, had published in 1915 a book opposing secret diplomacy: *Democracy and Diplomacy—A Plea for Popular Control of Foreign Policy* (Methuen).

could not bind its successors to adopt this procedure, and it was not accepted by the Conservative Government 1924–9[1]. The Labour administration 1929–31 reverted to the Ponsonby principles, then after 1931 the position became unclear. Sir Ivor Jennings recorded that the Ponsonby Rule 'has presumably not been followed (since 1931), although no formal announcement to that effect appears to have been made'.[2] But in October 1939, the Prime Minister (Neville Chamberlain) told the Commons that 'It is usual for treaties to be laid before the House for twenty-one days before ratification but in view of the exceptional circumstances, it is desired that the Anglo-French-Turkish Treaty should be ratified as soon as possible. It is therefore proposed to submit the treaty for His Majesty's signature at once and to arrange for the instruments of ratification to reach Ankara next week'.[3] A discussion on the constitutional position took place in the Lords on March 11, 1953,[4] and arose from dissatisfaction that the Sudan Agreement had not been available for debate before coming into effect. Viscount Swinton, the Government spokesman, stressed that there was nothing in British constitutional practice that corresponded to Senatorial ratification of treaties in the United States; if a treaty required ratification it was entirely a matter for the Government to decide whether to seek parliamentary consent before completing ratification. He added that treaties were, in fact, submitted to Parliament where they could not be implemented without legislation and when the importance of the treaty was so great that parliamentary agreement was politically desirable although not legally necessary.

Four years later, however, the Foreign Secretary, Selwyn Lloyd, accepted the Ponsonby Rule in relation to treaties requiring ratification and implied that this had been the position adopted by previous governments.[5] Thus the latest edition of Erskine May states that when a treaty requires ratification the Government 'do not usually proceed with ratification until a period of twenty-one days has elapsed from the date on which

[1] H. C. Deb., Vol. 179, col. 565 and Vol. 230, col. 408.
[2] *Cabinet Government* (Cambridge University Press, 1937), p. 374.
[3] H. C. Deb., Vol. 352, col. 1407.
[4] H. L. Deb., Vol. 180, cols. 1282–8.
[5] H. C. Deb., Vol. 579, cols. 370–1.

the text of such a treaty was laid before Parliament by Her Majesty's command'.[1] The word 'usually' permits modification of the practice in cases of emergency—as in 1939. The value of the delay is also limited in so far as it affects but a minority of diplomatic arrangements. No agreement constituted by an Exchange of Notes is ever stated by its terms to be subject to ratification. As to other forms of diplomatic agreement, of the 190 published in the Treaty series between 1960–4, only 27% contained a clause providing for compulsory ratification, 63% entered into force by virtue of signature alone and for the remaining 10% ratification was optional. The Ponsonby Rule also applies solely to treaties and does not extend to other forms of international action: in April, 1957, Britain withdrew from the optional compulsory jurisdiction clause of the Statute of the International Court without informing Parliament.[2]

In recent years there have been but few debates on treaties, partly because the number of formal treaties of first-class importance has been small. When there is broad agreement between Government and Opposition, the Foreign Office may welcome a debate as a demonstration of united national support for its policy: thus the 1954 Paris agreements on defence that led to the re-arming of Western Germany were approved by the Commons on a vote of 264 to 4 with the Opposition abstaining. Alternatively, as noted above, if the Opposition strongly opposes the Government's actions, there is no way of avoiding debate although this might possibly have to take place *after* the treaty had become operative. The present arrangements may well enable Ministers to avoid an awkward discussion on a treaty if their opponents are unwilling to make it a major issue; especially can this be so if objections to the treaty come mainly from government backbenchers.

Parliamentary debate on the terms of a treaty is almost always avoided before negotiations are completed: any debate could create embarrassment for our representatives at the negotiating table. There has, however, been one major exception to this rule for in 1951 Herbert Morrison, the Foreign Secretary, outlined the main provisions of the draft peace treaty with Japan which

---

[1] 17th ed., 1964, p. 274. This statement did not appear in earlier editions.
[2] H. C. Deb., Vol. 577, col. 491. See p. 52 *infra*.

was still under discussion.[1] The draft treaty was subsequently a subject of debate on the Second Reading of the Consolidated Fund Bill[2] which is a traditional opportunity for backbench M.P.s to raise topics of their own choice. As no prior notice had been given of the intention to discuss the draft treaty, no Foreign Office spokesman was present during the debate but the Government gave an undertaking that note would be taken of points made by Members.

DIPLOMATIC RECOGNITION

The Royal Prerogative also provides authority for the *de jure* or *de facto* recognition of foreign governments and the associated formalities governing the appointment and reception of diplomatic representatives. In 1851 Queen Victoria was able to force the resignation of the Foreign Secretary, Lord Palmerston, as he had expressed approval for the *coup d'état* by Louis Napoleon in a conversation with the French Ambassador without consulting either the Cabinet or the Queen. The right of the Monarch to express an opinion, or as Bagehot put it 'encourage, advise and warn', on affairs of state could not be maintained if action on important policy issues were taken without foreknowledge by the Queen. Palmerston's offence was acute since approval of a new regime touched directly upon the Royal Prerogative.

The Commons need not be consulted before a Cabinet decides to open or break off diplomatic relations with a state or a new regime. The precedents vary as to how a Government does behave. In May, 1927, Prime Minister Baldwin announced that relations with the Soviet Union would be broken off unless the Commons disapproved of this policy in the foreign affairs debate to be held two days later. In February, 1939, the Chamberlain Government accorded *de jure* recognition to the Franco regime in Spain four days after the Prime Minister had refused to make any statement on this subject in the Commons. This provoked a major parliamentary storm.[3] Questions of diplomatic recognition are more likely to stir party controversy than major issues of war and peace. Especially has this been true of the Soviet

[1] H. C. Deb., Vol. 490, cols. 630–6.
[2] H. C. Deb., Vol. 491, cols. 359–82.
[3] H. C. Deb., Vol. 344, cols. 1099–1222.

Union and Franco Spain; in the case of the Soviet Union, *de facto* acceptance came in 1921, *de facto* recognition was accepted by the Labour Government in 1924, this was withdrawn in 1927 and re-established by the second Labour Government in 1929. The normal policy of the British Government now is to recognize any regime which effectively controls a well-defined area of territory. Thus the Chinese Communist government was recognized in 1950.

Although the Commons have no right to prior consultation before decisions are made, questions relating to diplomatic representation are frequently raised in the Commons. Question-time is particularly suitable for a specific topic of this nature. In June, 1964, a Labour backbencher, W. N. Warbey, asked a question the purpose of which was to get the Government spokesman to reiterate that this country does not recognize the Chiang Kai-shek regime in Taiwan. In the following month another Labour Member, C. P. Mayhew, asked about the resumption of relations with the Somali Republic. These examples can be multiplied endlessly and they illustrate that the House of Commons does exercise constant scrutiny over the pattern of our diplomatic associations. Similarly, Parliament has no power to ratify the appointment of ambassadors as has the United States' Senate, but an appointment could be a subject of debate. However, parliamentary criticism of such nominations is rare since these posts are largely filled by career diplomats who are covered by the tradition of political neutrality in the civil service.

CHAPTER IV

Sources of Information

MEMBERS of Parliament cannot exercise effective influence and scrutiny over public business unless they are well informed. This proposition applies equally to domestic affairs and to foreign policy. However, knowledge of conditions abroad is more difficult to acquire. Close examination of foreign affairs debates in Parliament will reveal that some Members are better briefed than others on details of the issues under discussion. Partly this is because some Members take greater care to prepare their speeches; partly it will be because some Members have taken the trouble to open up additional avenues of communication which can provide them with specialized material.

Members, of course, can study world affairs through the same means as are available to the general public: they can listen to television and radio and read the press, books and specialized journals. But out legislators also enjoy special opportunities and facilities. Not least of these is their physical presence in Westminster; those who are near the seat of government should know more of current developments than those who merely observe from a distance. Besides the formal proceedings of debates and question-time, the process of informal conversation between Members, and between Members and Ministers, plays a valuable part in their education. There are also certain official free facilities and private means of aid available for Members who wish to use them. These can be divided into original sources of information and channels of information, but the distinction is not clear-cut.

OFFICIAL PUBLICATIONS

Traditionally, Members have been entitled to obtain information from the Government through a wide variety of returns and reports—in addition to the procedure of question-time. Thus they can have a free supply of a large number of official publications. This includes *Hansard* and its indexes, in the daily parts, the weekly edition and the bound volumes. It includes also the Votes and Proceedings, Acts, Bills and Parliamentary Papers of the current and two previous sessions. Members can also have a copy of older Papers if available and if needed for the discharge of their parliamentary duties. Where a document is particularly relevant to a debate, the Minister in charge must ensure that a reasonable number of copies are available and, where necessary, the document will be reprinted. The Stationery Office will also provide Members with a free copy of any non-parliamentary publication needed for his parliamentary duties; historical, technical and scientific works are excluded from this arrangement.[1] Not all these documents are supplied automatically. The Vote Office circulates to Members the Votes and Proceedings, *Hansard*, Public Bills, supplementary estimates, the financial statement and any other document which a Minister thinks to be of sufficient importance. Papers other than these are obtained on request. It appears that the appetite of Members for information is growing: in the session 1956/57 the Vote Office despatched 156,059 papers to Members, a figure which rose to 291,208 in 1962/63.[2]

The distinction between parliamentary papers and non-parliamentary publications is largely conventional but occasionally arbitrary.[3] The documents that have more immediate relevance to parliamentary business are known as parliamentary papers; they are indexed separately and are issued in bound sets for each session. Parliamentary papers are substantial in bulk and there are now about forty volumes every session with an average of over a thousand pages each. But by far the larger part of this material is concerned with domestic, economic and financial business: usually only three of the forty volumes are

[1] Rulings on the supply of publications to Members appear in *Hansard:* Vol. 556, cols. 1044–5 and Vol. 651, cols. 221–4. See also P. and G. Ford, *A Guide to Parliamentary Papers* (Blackwell, 1955), for an analysis of their contents and methods of classification.

[2] These figures exclude papers which are handed to Members across the counter of the Vote Office.

[3] These categories were created in 1921 to limit the cost of the free circulation of parliamentary papers. The Controller of the Stationery Office has the authority to decide whether a document shall be classified as parliamentary.

related to foreign affairs. The quantity of non-parliamentary papers issued by the Foreign Office is negligible.

Parliamentary papers dealing with foreign affairs have varied in their nature. The extent of these publications has depended on the attitude of each Foreign Secretary (or Prime Minister) towards publicity, the strength of their position in Parliament and on the nature of contemporary problems.[1] There is a general rule of diplomatic practice that information is not released officially about incomplete negotiations and, since the end of the nineteenth century, an increasing proportion of these parliamentary papers have recorded agreements already concluded with foreign governments. Sometimes the selection of documents published has been carefully edited to suppress material that might be embarrassing or inflammatory. After Castlereagh the tendency was to issue an increasing amount of information—a reflection of the strength of our international position and of the vigour and independence of mind in the post-1832 House of Commons. At this period some of the Blue Books appeared through ministerial initiative but others were produced as a result of an Address, or request, from either House of Parliament. Towards the end of the century the parliamentary papers became less informative. Instead, question-time in the Commons was used to extract information from Ministers since the growth of party discipline enabled Ministers to prevent unwelcome Addresses asking for papers on a delicate topic. Further, there developed an inclination to withhold information about relations with European powers which led eventually to secret diplomacy. Thus the Anglo-German Convention of 1898 was never communicated to Parliament and the secret articles of the Anglo-French Treaty of 1904 were suppressed for seven years. After 1918 the demand for 'open covenants, openly arrived at' had but a limited effect on the contents of official publications for Lloyd George tended to use the Press as a more immediate and effective means of publicity. In later years, of course, radio and television have largely replaced the Press.

[1] This paragraph is based on H. Temperley and L. M. Penson, *A Century of Diplomatic Blue Books 1814–1914* (Cambridge University Press, 1938) and R. Vogel, *A Breviate of British Diplomatic Blue Books 1919–1939* (McGill University Press, 1963). See also A. J. P. Taylor, *The Struggle for Mastery in Europe 1848–1914* (O.U.P., 1954), pp. 569–71.

However, it became more usual after 1918 to publish treaties prior to ratification. Also some of the documents issued seemed to be designed not so much to inform Parliament but to counteract propaganda by the Opposition and so strengthen the Government's position with the public.[1] Austen Chamberlain's cautious policy on publications led to renewed protests about secret diplomacy, especially when reports of negotiations leaked into newspapers abroad. The parliamentary papers of the late nineteen-thirties show little of the diplomacy of the Neville Chamberlain–Hitler era: no explanatory Blue Books were issued covering British guarantees to Greece, Roumania and Poland in 1939 although these arrangements were not confidential and, indeed, secrecy would have defeated their purpose. Naturally, Governments dislike issuing material that may aggravate a delicate situation. In May, 1966, Edward Heath, the Leader of the Opposition, asked if all papers relevant to our position in Aden might be published: the Foreign Secretary, Michael Stewart, replied that this would involve publication of documents concerning South Arabia for a long period, 'For a variety of reasons one would want to consider that carefully.'[2]

Today parliamentary papers on foreign policy are essentially formal—mostly they comprise the texts of treaties, conventions and other international agreements entered into by the Government. Correspondence with foreign governments is still sometimes published. A few reports from international bodies are included, the United Nations and its specialized agencies, particularly UNESCO. Before 1960 the report of the Council of Europe was issued as a parliamentary paper. Summaries are also produced regularly listing the treaties and other agreements that the United Kingdom has ratified, accepted or withdrawn from in recent months. It is, of course, vital that such information be made available to Members. Nevertheless, many of these documents do little to aid understanding of major issues of foreign policy.

The texts of treaties, agreements etc. are commonly issued twice, after signature and again after coming into effect. An agreement not yet in force is included in the 'Country' or

[1] Eg. the Reports on conditions in Russia: 1919 Cmd. 8 liii, 1920 Cmd. 1041 xxv, 1921 Cmd. 1240 xliii.
[2] H. C. Deb., Vol. 728, col. 934.

'Miscellaneous' series of official publications: agreements in force are included in the 'Treaty' series. In the former case only the English text of an agreement is usually given, but in the Treaty Series all the original languages of signature are reproduced. A treaty subject to ratification requires dual publication since, under the Ponsonby rule, presentation to Parliament is necessary at least twenty-one sitting days before it is ratified.[1] In addition treaties, agreements etc. may not be enforceable in this country until domestic legislation has been enacted. Thus there can be a considerable time gap between signature and implementation. An agreement between the United Kingdom and Spain about air services was made in July, 1950, published in December, 1950,[2] ratified in January, 1960, and appeared again as a parliamentary paper in March, 1961.[3] A Universal Postal Convention was completed at Ottawa in October, 1957, published as a parliamentary paper in December, 1958,[4] ratified by the United Kingdom in July, 1959, and republished in December, 1960.[5] Such examples can be multiplied endlessly. There may be excellent reasons for delay in ratification or implementation of an agreement—but why the subsequent delay in its publication?

Such delay is particularly serious on actions that do not require ratification and a minor parliamentary storm broke over one such incident in 1957. In April of that year the British Government introduced additional reservations on the extent to which it was prepared to accept the jurisdiction of the International Court of Justice. These were not made public until August during the summer recess and the Commons were unable to debate the matter before November. The Foreign Secretary, Selwyn Lloyd, agreed ultimately that the delay in publication had been 'regrettable',[6]

TRIPS ABROAD

International travel is invaluable for promoting understanding of conditions abroad through the opportunities it provides for

[1] See pp. 43–5 *supra*.   [2] 1950–1, Cmd. 8112, xxxiii.
[3] 1960–1, Cmnd. 1297, xxxiv.   [4] 1958–9, Cmnd. 576, xxxi.
[5] 1960–1, Cmnd. 1218, xxxiii.
[6] 1956–7, Cmnd. 249, xxxi and H. C. Deb., Vol. 577, cols. 472–5, Vol. 578, cols. 1144–6 and Vol. 579, cols. 370–1.

observation and conversation. Many Members of Parliament travel quite extensively. Their journeyings may be wholly or partly for holiday purposes; some are connected with their business or professional interests as company directors or journalists. Some Members have previously lived abroad for substantial periods of time, usually in military service or as colonial officials. Such experience is of less value for it becomes out of date; moreover the Armed Forces do not necessarily provide an environment conducive to political sensitivity. Indeed, if these limitations are not appreciated, impressions gathered in earlier years can be a positive hindrance to contemporary understanding. Of greater use is the stream of official parliamentary delegations to other countries in connexion with the Council of Europe, the North Atlantic Treaty Organization, the Commonwealth Parliamentary Association and the Inter-Parliamentary Union. These official arrangements are helpful to Members in two ways; not only are expenses paid but they permit absence from Westminster when Parliament is sitting without incurring displeasure from the Whips. The delegations reflect party strengths in the Commons but the membership can be adjusted by using Peers so that the Government majority is unaffected.

Each year a strong delegation goes to Strasbourg to attend the Consultative Assembly of the Council of Europe. This group is about twenty in number and is drawn mainly from the Commons, but a few Lords are included also. The political composition of the delegation reflects party strengths in the House of Commons. Since it was created in 1949 the Council of Europe has disappointed the federalist hopes of many of its founders and the Assembly has but limited advisory functions. Nevertheless, the Assembly is still a useful focal point for the discussion, formally and otherwise, of contemporary European problems.[1]

The NATO Parliamentarians' Conference has met annually

[1] For a study of voting behaviour by national delegations at the Consultative Assembly and at the Assembly of Western European Union see Peter H. Merkl, *Journal of Conflict Resolution* (1964), Vol. 8, pp. 50–64. Western European Union was initiated in 1955 to discuss matters of defence policy which are expressly excluded from the functions of the Council of Europe: the members of W.E.U. are Britain, France, Germany, Italy and the Benelux countries.

since 1955.[1] Its object as officially defined is 'to strengthen political understanding and co-operation among member countries and, in their respective legislatures, give active proof of their interest in the problems and the development of the Alliance.' No member of a Government can join the delegations to the Conference which makes policy recommendations in very general terms to the ministerial North Atlantic Council and to member governments. Five separate committees have been formed to deal with political, military, economic, scientific and cultural affairs. The Conference is a useful additional meeting-place for the discussion of international problems: there is little likelihood that it will exert profound influence over NATO policy.

The Commonwealth Parliamentary Association was founded in 1911 (the original title was the Empire Parliamentary Association) to facilitate the exchange of information, closer understanding and more frequent intercourse between parliamentarians of the constituent countries. Visits are arranged in both directions. British delegations going abroad are usually small, with about six members, but two or three delegations may be away simultaneously. These trips are dominated by the Commons but occasionally a couple of peers are included. Members of both Houses can join the CPA on an individual basis and a large majority of the Commons do so.

Very similar to the CPA are the membership and pattern of visits arranged through the British Group of the Inter-Parliamentary Union. The IPU was founded in 1889 to promote the cause of peace through the development of international co-operation and understanding. It helped to establish the International Court and, in general, encourages members of legislatures throughout the world to give support to the work of international organizations. Membership extends beyond countries normally considered democratic and includes states as diverse as Spain and the Soviet Union. In addition to arranging visits to and from other countries, the British Group of the IPU sends a delegation to the annual conference of the organization and another to the annual meeting of its Council. Linked to the

---

[1] The British Government was originally hostile to this organisation. However, two ex-Ministers, Walter Elliot (Con.) and Sir Geoffrey de Freitas (Lab.) played a large part in securing British participation and support.

British Group are no fewer than twenty-four sub-groups that exist to promote better relations between the United Kingdom and a particular foreign country. Some of the sub-groups are reasonably active and organize discussions, dinners and other social occasions, often in conjunction with the respective Embassies; others are largely inactive, if not moribund. The 1965 Report of the Anglo-Bulgarian Group is as follows: 'There has been little activity during the year and the Group hopes for an increase in membership.'

The visitations arranged through the CPA and the IPU have a higher social content than those connected with the Council of Europe and NATO. There is less formal political discussion and much time is spent on carefully planned tours to places of interest and on official hospitality, all in conditions of some luxury. How far such trips help to provide a realistic appreciation of conditions elsewhere must be a matter of doubt. It is notable that many of the Members who take a prominent part in foreign policy discussions in the Commons seem to have little interest in the IPU. These activities receive financial support from the Treasury, but the Government does not decide who shall be asked to join the various trips abroad. However, the Whips do have influence over the nominations and it may be that they are unlikely to favour Members who are excessively outspoken or potentially rebellious.

Occasionally Members travel abroad at the invitation of foreign governments or other foreign organizations and their expenses may be met, at least in part, by their hosts. Such visits can be arranged in order to present Members with information or a particular point of view on an international problem that may concern the British legislature. In the nineteen-thirties some Members visited Budapest at the invitation of a newspaper closely associated with the Hungarian Government. 'They came back having not only enjoyed themselves but having been made fully aware of the views of the Hungarian Government on the question of the revision of the Treaty of Trianon.'[1] At the same period Members of all parties went on sponsored trips to Nazi Germany. More recently Members on both sides of the House have been to the United States, the Soviet Union and the Central African Federation on a similar basis. If on returning home

[1] The Solicitor General, Sir Dingle Foot, H.C. Deb., Vol. 709, col. 615.

Members support the policy of their erstwhile hosts, they may lay themselves open to the insinuation that their views have been influenced by the hospitality received. No doubt any gibe of this kind would be utterly baseless. But it may be the path of wisdom for Members not to make sponsored trips to centres of international tension.[1]

INSTITUTIONAL ASSISTANCE

Members also obtain a great amount of help and information from a variety of organizations concerned with public affairs which tend to be sited conveniently close to the Palace of Westminster. Chief among these are the headquarters organizations of the major political parties.

The Conservative Research Department has an independent status within the Conservative Party and is housed separately from the Central Office. The CRD produces a number of pamphlets for public sale, but which are used largely by Members, prospective candidates and party workers. Those on foreign affairs often contain factual information supported by quotations from recent speeches of party leaders and serve to indicate the official pattern of Conservative thinking. A confidential duplicated brief is produced in advance for each major debate in the Commons and serves to give Conservative Members a basis for supporting the Party's view. The CRD staff also provide secretarial assistance for the committees formed by Members to study particular topics.[2]

[1] To imply that a Member's performance of his *parliamentary* duties had been influenced by hospitality would be a breach of parliamentary privilege. In the Christmas recess of 1964 W. Warbey (Lab. Ashfield) visited North Vietnam and his hotel bill in Hanoi was paid for by the Fatherland Front, a Communist organisation. This fact was noted by *The Spectator* and *The Daily Telegraph* in commenting upon Warbey's support for the North Vietnamese government. Warbey complained in the Commons that these articles constituted a breach of privilege by suggesting 'he was not a witness of truth but a bribed spokesman for a foreign government.' (H.C. Deb., Vol. 707, cols. 43-4.) His complaint was later debated and rejected, the Solicitor General advising the House that as *The Spectator* and *The Daily Telegraph* had related their comments to Warbey's general political activities and not specifically to his actions as a Member of Parliament, no breach of privilege had been committed. (H.C. Deb., Vol. 709, cols. 576-642).

[2] See pp. 133-4.

Inevitably, the activities of the CRD are affected by whether the Party is in office or in opposition. When in office, the research officers' discussions with party leaders will tend to be restricted to the discussion of public presentation of Government policy, and of public reaction to it. These are essentially political matters regarded by civil servants as being outside their province. Backbench Members will come to the research staff with requests for information which may be used in parliamentary debate: as opposed to the service provided by the Commons' Library staff, the information may be supplied with a political slant or bite in it. A situation of some delicacy can arise if a backbencher asks for material about a topic whereon his views are known to diverge from those of the party leadership. The research staff may well be unhappy about helping to provide ammunition that they suspect is to be used against their own Ministers. Probably such requests obtain a minimum of co-operation.

When the Party is in opposition, the Research Department has greater responsibility and more opportunity for initiative. The 'Shadow' Ministers, deprived of civil service aid, need more assistance and are in more regular contact with Party staff. They require material for speeches inside and outside Parliament. The research staff may suggest lines of attack on Government policy and useful openings for parliamentary questions. Much less time is available to give attention to backbenchers who will be encouraged to use the resources of the Commons' Library. The CRD becomes more deeply involved in the formulation of Party policy, and the strains on the organization are heavy.

Only four out of a research staff of thirty specialize in foreign affairs. They obtain material from a range of books, journals and official publications from home and abroad. They maintain links with the Royal Institute of International Affairs, the Institute of Strategic Studies and various embassies. Occasionally a member of the foreign affairs section travels, e.g. to the Council of Europe meetings or to a gathering of NATO parliamentarians. But the proportion of the CRD resources allocated to foreign issues is low. This may be a reflection of the amount of time Parliament spends on international problems, or it could arise from a conviction among Conservative leaders that foreign affairs can be dealt with by experienced statesmen and diplomats and does not demand 'back-room boys' investigation. There is also a feeling in the Conservative hierarchy that foreign policy is not very significant in terms of winning votes.

The Labour Party has a rather smaller research staff than the Conservatives, although the numbers specializing in foreign affairs are similar. Again, the pattern of work is affected by the electoral fortunes of the Party. In opposition the research staff should be more in touch with Shadow Ministers, assisting in the preparation of speeches and suggesting themes for political attack. Between 1945 and 1963 the International Department at Transport House had an uneven, sometimes uneasy status in the party organization. More than once the post of Head of the Department was left vacant for several months, suggesting that Party leaders did not regard it of vital importance. Gaitskell, as Party Leader, tended to ignore Transport House and had other sources of information. Wilson, when Leader of the Opposition, used the research staff more fully. Other Shadow Ministers have varied in their attitude: often they required factual information on specific matters or quotations from earlier debates designed to score debating points off opponents by imputing inconsistency —a rather useless gambit played by Members of all parties. However, one front-bench spokesman on foreign affairs in the nineteen-fifties asked the research staff not merely for help but for drafts of speeches; no doubt he subsequently amended and polished what he was given. Another told me that he never used the research staff since he knew more of foreign affairs than they did. Limited assistance was also made available to backbenchers expecting to speak in a foreign affairs debate, if they were broadly in support of Party policy.

Transport House clearly has insufficient resources to provide a research service for all Labour Members. A duplicated newsheet is issued each week containing factual information and quotations from pronouncements by Party Leaders; it is intended mainly for Members, parliamentary candidates and party workers. Inevitably any digest of material is selective and tends to imply conclusions. So these information sheets, the intellectual quality of which is not high, tend to propagate official policy on any matters in dispute within the Party. The Labour research staff also keep in touch with European democratic socialist parties.

In 1960–1 a curious situation arose. The 1960 Party Confer-
ence had accepted the policy of unilateral nuclear disarmament,
a resolution which was opposed and ignored by Gaitskell as
Leader, and by the majority of Labour Members of Parliament.
But a significant minority of Labour Members supported the
Conference resolution while others tried to sustain an uneasy
neutrality between the two camps. Some leading anti-Gaitskell
Members claimed the right to be briefed with information and
argument to support the view of the Conference: since the
Conference theoretically determines Party policy this claim
succeeded. So for a year the research staff were preparing in the
same office diametrically opposed briefs on foreign and defence
policy.

The impact of a research department depends greatly on the
nature of the personal relationships between the research staff
and leading politicians. Where these are close, the researchers
may travel more and be influential. In office, Ministers use party
headquarters for advice on issues of party propaganda but not
for official policy. Party researchers tend to relapse into an
information service providing ammunition to help the followers
to give aid to their leaders.

Many institutions, other than political parties, supply information to Members. They can be divided into two broad
categories—the pressure groups and the (relatively) disinterested.
It is perhaps indelicate and inaccurate to describe foreign
embassies as pressure groups, but they are always ready to
explain their government's viewpoint to any Members willing to
listen. Other pressure group activity will be examined in Chapter
VII; inevitably, information from such sources is potentially
slanted with a particular end in view. However, Members do not
necessarily draw the same conclusions from material as those
who provide it. The disinterested sources have more of an
academic flavour. A few Members attend specialized seminars
at the London School of Economics or are in touch with the
work of the Institute of Strategic Studies. Some Conservatives
and fewer Labour Members join the Royal Institute of International Affairs, which provides a library and a specialized
press cuttings service at Chatham House. It also arranges
lecture meetings and study groups. Yet the overall use of these
facilities by Members appears to be small. Independent research

workers and university staff have more time to read and think than politicians, but the latter are curiously loath to seek advantage from academic contacts. Members who are journalists benefit from their connexions with the Press, including foreign correspondents. The Research Division of the Foreign Office will also provide factual information so long as it is not required for a party political purpose. Finally, many meetings are held in the Palace of Westminster addressed by politicians from all parts of the world, notably the more troubled areas. Either they are party gatherings, or are arranged by some extra-parliamentary organization with the co-operation of sympathetic Members. The importance of these meetings is considerable. Their privacy permits a degree of frankness which would be impossible, if not dangerous, elsewhere. And being in the Palace it is convenient for Members to attend, especially when they are kept by the Whips in anticipation of a division in the Chamber.

THE COMMONS' LIBRARY

The Library of the House of Commons is an institution of long standing but it is only in recent years that its services in providing information for M.P.s have developed substantially. In 1818 the first Librarian was appointed to care for a small but growing collection of documents and to make them available to Members.[1] Thomas Vardon told a Select Committee in 1835 'there is no subject connected with parliamentary business . . . on which I am not called upon to afford instant information'.[2] This statement was an excellent recognition of obligation but for a century after Vardon gave his evidence the Commons' Library retained the atmosphere of a gentleman's club in which M.P.s read, wrote letters or sometimes dozed. Then in 1945 a Select Committee undertook a general reappraisal of the function of the Library and defined its purpose thus: 'To supply Members with information rapidly on any of the multifarious matters that come before the House or to which their attentions are drawn by

[1] David Menhennet, 'The Library of the House of Commons' in *Political Quarterly* (1965). Vol. 36, pp. 323–32.
[2] *Library of the House of Commons.* Standing Committee Report; 1835 (104) xviii.

their parliamentary duties.'[1] So that the Library could be made more useful to Members the Committee recommended the appointment of two Research Assistants, an important development which led subsequently to the division of the library into two departments; the Parliamentary Division cares for the main Library in a magnificent suite of rooms overlooking the River and the Research Division occupies humbler quarters below searching out information needed by Members.

The Library stock is now of the order of 100,000 volumes together with a large collection of British official publications and documents and reports issued by the Council of Europe, the European Economic Community and other international organizations. A large number of official United States documents are obtained as well as many Government publications from Commonwealth countries. The Library is a deposit library for United Nations publications. Further, it takes about 1,600 periodicals and 100 newspapers from a wide variety of countries. Thus there is a vast amount of material available for Members about contemporary events, but it is of equal importance that this material should be sifted and analysed so that Members can be readily directed to items that concern them. Clearly, this is a task almost without end. Within the limits of the available resources a great deal is done to facilitate the Members' search for information. A select press-cutting service is maintained for home and foreign affairs. Visible strip indexes are provided for major topics which show references to recent parliamentary debates and official publications dealing with each subject. Much of the material relating to events abroad surrounds the International Affairs Desk, at which a graduate library assistant, aided by a clerk and a typist, does her best to meet the requirements of Members. Some queries can be satisfied immediately: others require a little research and are answered by correspondence.

The Research Division prepares reference sheets containing bibliographies and statistical memoranda that may be of use in connexion with future debates. But its main task is to deal with Members' questions of a kind that cannot be answered by rapid reference to standard sources. Often the research staff must seek what is required from outside the Library and they gather

[1] *Library* (*House of Commons*). Sel. Cttee. Report, para. 5; 1945–6 (35) viii.

information from Government Departments, other public authorities and specialized libraries. If the information is required for a forthcoming debate, the research staff must do the best they can within a time-limit that is often as short as 48 hours. Normally, Members can be provided only with material already published and the Library is in no position to obtain information that is confidential to Ministers and their civil service advisers. Occasionally, and this applies to foreign affairs, it is possible to get from a Government Department a document in the 'grey zone' category which is neither published nor confidential.

What are the proper limits to aid given to Members? In 1960 the Advisory Committee[1] decided that the Library should not 'brief' Members,[2] but the concept of 'briefing' is open to interpretation. Obviously the research staff must not write speeches for Members, yet the material they produce is often incorporated in speeches in the Chamber. Some Members use this service to gather information to buttress a pre-determined attitude: others seek help in connexion with speaking engagements outside Parliament. As a result the work of the Research Division is of extraordinary variety, but consists of fairly rapid information collection rather than 'research' in the academic sense of that word. At all times the researchers must be scrupulously accurate. Their duties—which may often be exasperating—are, in fact, carried out with an acute sense of professional dedication.

Members make surprisingly little use of these facilities. In 1960, the last year for which published figures are available, 274 Members between them asked the Research Division for information 615 times and put a further 329 queries to the associated statistical section.[3] It seems that pressure on the Research Division is increasing and contemporary figures are doubtless higher. Even so, the average of 1·5 queries per Member in 1960

[1] The Library is under the control of the Speaker who had an advisory committee of Members to assist him on matters of policy between the years 1834–61 and 1922–65. This committee had no official status and no means of pressing advice as it could not report to the Commons. In 1965 there was a major reallocation of responsibility for the internal services of Parliament. The Library is now supervised by a sub-committee of a new Select Committee on House of Commons Services.

[2] *Estimates.* Sel. Cttee. 2nd Report, *House of Commons Library*, para. 8; 1960–1 (168) v.

[3] *Estimates.* Sel. Cttee. 10th Special Report, p. 4; 1960–1 (246) vi.

was scarcely excessive. The resources of the Division are correspondingly small with eight graduates on its staff, or one to eighty Members. No translation facilities are available, a service which is essential to the comprehensive study of foreign affairs. Were the demands of Members to increase, presumably the Division would be expanded: growth should make it more efficient as its staff could specialize more narrowly and develop detailed knowledge of the sources of information relevant to a restricted range of topics.

The legislative reference service of the Library of Congress has a staff of 200 and an annual appropriation exceeding £700,000. In contrast, the Commons' Library has a staff of thirty-six and the Civil Estimates for 1965-6 authorize expenditure of £56,000 on staff salaries and a further £9,000 on the purchase and maintenance of books. No doubt, the present generation of Members would regard Library provision on anything approaching the American scale as unnecessary and probably improper. But there is now a strong demand among Members that Library services should be improved and it is noteworthy that the Librarian recommended in 1965 that the International Affairs Desk should be given top priority in any future expansion of Library facilities.[1]

THE LACK OF INFORMATION

In spite of—or perhaps because of—the facilities available to Members of Parliament, it is difficult to resist the conclusion that many are ill-informed about international problems. Even a front bench spokesman who leaves his prepared brief may betray ignorance or forgetfulness.[2] For backbenchers the various

[1] In evidence to the Select Committee on the Palace of Westminster: 1964-5 (285) q. 313.

[2] An extreme example of this kind is the argument that developed in 1954 between Sir Winston Churchill, then Prime Minister, and Clement Attlee, then leader of the Opposition, over whether the Labour Government should have taken more vigorous action in 1946 to prevent the passage of the MacMahon Act through the United States' Congress. Both participants in this extraordinary incident appeared to believe that the MacMahon Act ended the British veto over United States' use of atomic weapons: in fact, the Act was concerned with the communication of information about atomic research. This forgetfulness was, no doubt, due to the advanced age of both party leaders. See Lord Moran, *Churchill: the Struggle for Survival* (Constable, 1966), pp. 534–8 and H.C. Deb., Vol. 526, cols. 51–5.

information channels discussed in this chapter are unsatisfactory being formalized, superficial, partisan or inadequate. The small resources of the Research Division of the Commons' Library reflect, in part, the modest claims for assistance made by Members. Naturally, Ministers and 'Shadow' Ministers have other aids, although it is not unknown for them to use the Library. Perhaps some Members have never become accustomed to the idea that a reference service is available for them or are inhibited by the manifest sparsity of its staff. Surely no one now holds the nineteenth-century view that all essential information is made available through official publications, a view which, granted the scale of nineteenth-century Blue Books, was then not unreasonable. No doubt, in years past Members were restrained from asking for better facilities for reasons analogous to those that held back demands for better salaries—reluctance to vote benefits for themselves that must, of course, be financed through higher taxation. And the Conservative Party has been loath to accept the concept of a backbench Member being a professional politician expected to devote his whole time to public affairs.

There is now a movement among Members to press for better Library facilities. But this is only a part of the wider question of improving working conditions for Members. The Palace of Westminster was not designed as the nerve centre of a vigorous democracy: its modernization will be a painful process involving not only heavy financial cost but also breaches of tradition. Meanwhile Members suffer lack of office space and secretarial aid. If backbenchers are to be better 'briefed' they also need research assistants; a few already manage to pay for this kind of help from their own resources. However, tradition limits the usefulness of these assistants since they are barred from the Library.

Even if the state were more generous in giving help to Members, there would still be two major barriers to their fuller appreciation of foreign policy and other issues. The first is time. Christopher Hollis, formerly a Conservative Member, has described parliamentary life as a ceaseless round of activity which leaves Members little time to read books.[1] No doubt, this is an exaggeration. Yet Members who devote the greater part

[1] *Can Parliament Survive?* (Hollis and Carter, 1949), pp. 69–70.

of their energies to public affairs can still absorb but a limited amount of information, and foreign affairs is only one sector of the whole field of public policy. If more facilities were made available, the most that could be expected is that a backbencher willing to specialize could attain a fair degree of expertise on his chosen subject, roughly parallel to that now achieved by official Opposition spokesmen.

The other barrier is the reluctance of Ministers to provide information. It is true that the number of formal refusals is low, partly because Ministers are shielded by the pattern of parliamentary activity and partly because Members are insufficiently insistent. The most glaring example of information suppression is the refusal of Ministers to agree to an enquiry into the Suez incident, especially into the alleged collusion with France and Israel. Consequently it is impossible for Parliament or the general public to make a balanced judgment on this episode. This type of situation makes a mockery of democracy. It is obvious that every move made in a moment of crisis cannot be immediately revealed. But if revelation must always wait for thirty years (up to 1966 it was fifty years) before the public records are made available, then British statesmen may be able to suppress damaging information until long after their retirement. Since diplomacy offers exceptional opportunities for concealment, this situation is most likely to arise in connexion with foreign policy.

Britain has a valuable tradition of investigation into public scandals, but Conservative Ministers would not agree that Suez falls into the same category as the Profumo incident. However, the Dardanelles Commission provides an adequate precedent for investigation into the actions of Ministers in the development of a particular policy.[1]

Another buttress to executive secrecy is the Official Secrets Acts. Their application to Members was reviewed in 1938. Duncan Sandys, then the young Conservative Member for Norwood, submitted privately to the Secretary of State for War the draft of a parliamentary question which was based on confidential information about the nation's aircraft defences. Sandys subsequently complained to Parliament that pressure had been put on him to reveal his source of information. This

[1] First Report of the Dardanelles Commission; 1917–18, Cd. 8490, x.

led to a Select Committee enquiry which reported that Members were not entitled to solicit the disclosure of confidential material but that Members, in fact, sometimes did obtain such information and it would affect their parliamentary duties if they did not. The extent of a Member's immunity from the Official Secrets Acts has not been precisely defined and the Committee recommended that the Acts should not be used to impede Members from carrying out their parliamentary activities.[1]

Perhaps the most serious aspect of the lack of information for Members is that it has not been recognized as a problem of our parliamentary institutions. Until recently there has been no public discussion of the matter. The need for research and information in Government Departments was accepted by the Haldane Committee half-a-century ago.[2] Yet Parliament tends to continue on an amateur basis, although probably few Members would now subscribe to the view of Commander Bower that a Member should be able to keep abreast of current affairs by studying the press for half-an-hour a day.[3] Obviously Ministers will not urge that backbenchers ought to be briefed in order to subject the Government to more searching scrutiny. Members themselves may well have a natural unwillingness to publicize the shortcomings of their knowledge, although these result not from personal failings but from the pattern of the parliamentary system. The new and younger Members now seem ready to face the problem more realistically.

[1] *Official Secrets Acts.* Select Committee Report; 1938–9 (101) viii.
[2] *Machinery of Government.* Committee Report, pp. 22–35, 1918, Cd. 9230, xii.
[3] Letter to *The Times*, July 24, 1957. Commander Bower was Conservative Member for Cleveland 1931–45.

CHAPTER V

Parliamentary Debates

THE purpose of this chapter is to review the opportunities that Parliament enjoys for the discussion of foreign policy. Inevitably, what follows must include some description of the rules governing the use of parliamentary time, of their evolution towards the present system, and especially of the balance of initiative between Ministers and backbenchers. The central historical feature is the increased Government dominance over the pattern of parliamentary business due to the widening scope of the affairs of state and the growing strength of party discipline and therefore of cabinet authority. At the commencement of the nineteenth century only one day in a Commons' week was reserved for the Government, but in 1837 Ministers took a second day and in 1852 a third day. Further restrictions on backbenchers came in 1902 when it was agreed that Government business should have precedence at all sittings save on some Fridays and some other half-days. During war-time and other periods of pressure, private members' time has disappeared completely. There have also been various changes in the arrangements since 1902, but as from the session 1950–1 twenty Fridays have been available for backbenchers and four extra half-days were added in 1959.

Although the opportunities for backbench initiative have been drastically reduced, the traditional rights of the Opposition have been largely unaffected. It may at any time put down a censure motion criticising some aspect(s) of minsterial policy: such a challenge the Government must accept by finding time to debate the motion. Twenty-six days each session are allocated to the Committee of Supply when, in theory, the Commons—minus the Speaker—discuss the supply of money to the Crown by considering the annual estimates of expenditure. By convention, the subjects for these discussions are decided by the Opposition. Other procedures which enable the Opposition and back-benchers to influence the course of parliamentary business will be described below, and although the Government controls the majority of time it does so in a flexible manner. Subject to the over-riding need of Ministers to carry through their legislative programme, the Government will try to meet the wishes of the House in planning the pattern of its work.

Foreign affairs give rise to a relatively small amount of contentious legislation: the majority of time devoted to this subject is spent on general debates, questions and ministerial statements[1] which perform a variety of purposes. When Parliament is sitting they enable it to be kept informed of the latest international developments; they provide publicity for explanations of ministerial policy; they enable the Cabinet to discern trends in Opposition opinion;[2] they create a focus of scrutiny for ministerial actions; they enable Ministers to answer criticism; they register parliamentary support for Government policies. The need for the Cabinet to obtain parliamentary support is a curious combination of fact and fiction. It is fact in the sense that it occurs regularly and must continue if the essential democratic element in British government is to remain. It is fiction since the Government acts in advance of parliamentary sanction which, because of party loyalty, is virtually automatic.

FOREIGN OFFICE MINISTERS

The replies to parliamentary debates and questions are given by Ministers holding appointments at the Foreign Office, together with the Prime Minister. The number of Foreign Office Ministers has grown substantially since the end of the last war. Before 1948 the regular pattern was that of two Ministers, the Secretary of State for Foreign Affairs and a Parliamentary Under-Secretary. (Between 1918 and 1953 there was also a Secretary for Overseas Trade in charge of a separate department but responsible both to the Foreign Secretary and the President of the Board of Trade.) It was also the usual practice for one of

---

[1] The following chapter provides a detailed case-study of the attention given by Parliament to foreign affairs in the session 1962–3.

[2] Ministers are made aware of the opinions of their own party supporters by other less formal means: see pp. 133–43 *infra*.

the Foreign Office Ministers to be in the Commons and the other in the Lords. However, from 1940 to 1948 both Ministers were in the Commons, a situation that was ended by the nomination of a second Under-Secretary from the Lords. In 1950 a fourth appointment was added, this time of a Minister of State, a new rank intermediate in status between the Foreign Secretary and the Junior Ministers. A fifth appointment came in 1952 with a second Minister of State: five Ministers, including one in the Upper House, continued to be the usual Foreign Office quota until 1964. Wilson's Labour Government then had six Foreign Office Ministers: the Foreign Secretary, four Ministers of State (two in the Lords) and one Under-Secretary (also in the Lords). The two Ministers of State in the Lords had special duties: Lord Caradon represented the British Government at the United Nations and Lord Chalfont was given responsibility for disarmament.

It would be nice to think that the threefold increase in Foreign Office Ministers in less than twenty years was due to great developments in the vigour and authority of parliamentary debates on foreign affairs. Unhappily such an explanation would be fanciful. The truth is that we need more Ministers because there are ever more conferences and diplomatic gatherings at which the Government must be represented at a high level. The world of diplomacy is very conscious of status: to send a Parliamentary Under-Secretary to an international gathering will be taken as a lack of interest by the British Government, but to send a Minister of State is indicative of attention and concern.

The great argument about Foreign Office representation in Parliament has been whether the Foreign Secretary should be drawn from the Lords or the Commons. That he now normally comes from the Commons is symbolic of the growing democratic spirit in British government. During the nineteenth centry it was common for the Foreign Secretary to be a member of the Upper House: from 1868 to 1905 the office was always held by a peer. Contemporary comment regarded this as a convenient and proper arrangement. The nature of Foreign Office work, it was argued, was such that more matters had to receive attention at ministerial level and less could be left to the sole discretion of permanent servants. Thus the pressure of official business made it difficult for the Foreign Secretaryship to be combined with membership of the elected Chamber. It was also claimed, with equally dubious justification, that since all sections of political opinion were generally agreed on the objectives of foreign policy, there was less need for the Foreign Secretary to be personally responsible to the Commons. Sir Sidney Low, writing in 1904, was of the opinion that the 'Secretary of State for Foreign Affairs ought to be, and usually is, a member of a great aristocratic house.'[1] His view was based on the theory that members of the great land-owning families were most likely to have the qualities of character needed to undertake successfully the high responsibilities of the Foreign Office. Sir Sidney Low put the claims of the aristocracy in this way: 'The House of Lords makes it possible to bring in a certain number of men of a different stamp, men who are responsible to Parliament, without being at the mercy of the ballot, and who, from their training and position, may often have qualities which are difficult to find among those who have risen to prominence in an elective Chamber.'[2] A. Lawrence Lowell in his classic study *The Government of England*, first published in 1908, also felt it was difficult for the Foreign Secretary to sit in the Commons, but his case was based on burden of work, not the merits of aristocracy.[3]

Sir Edward Grey's unprecedentedly long tenure at the Foreign Office, 1905–16, effectively killed the pressure of business argument, while the wisdom and claims to authority of hereditary title-holders became acutely controversial after 1909. The objections to secret diplomacy and the demand for greater public knowledge and scrutiny of the development of foreign policy were also incompatible with the idea that the Foreign Secretary should be closeted away in the Lords. Since 1905 there have been four Foreign Secretaries in the Upper House; Lord Curzon 1919–24, Lord Reading, for a few months in 1931, Lord Halifax 1938–40 and Lord Home 1960–3. The decline of the Lord's authority was officially recognized when Baldwin rather than Lord Curzon was appointed Prime Minister in 1923, and thus was established the convention that the Prime Minister

---

[1] *The Governance of England* (T. Fisher Unwin), p. 252.
[2] *Ibid.* p. 251.
[3] Vol. 1, p. 87 (Macmillan).

must belong to the elected Chamber. In 1938 the Opposition argued that this practice should extend also to the Foreign Secretaryship, and the appointment of Lord Halifax was criticized, not on personal grounds, but as a matter of constitutional principle.[1]

The strength of a new convention of the constitution can be demonstrated only if an influential desire to ignore it is overcome. By this test the idea that the Foreign Secretary must belong to the Commons appeared to be firmly established by 1960. In 1955 the Prime Minister, Sir Anthony Eden, wished to appoint Lord Salisbury to the Foreign Secretaryship as he had had far greater experience of foreign affairs than other candidates for the post. Sir Anthony's memoirs,[2] published in 1960, contain a full statement of why he thought it impossible for the Foreign Secretary to be in the Lords. Important statements on foreign affairs could not be made to the Commons by a Junior Minister. A Minister of Cabinet rank would have to represent the Government in all important debates and—in Sir Anthony's view—that would have to be the Prime Minister himself. Sir Anthony was unwilling, quite rightly, to take on this added burden. Nor would a Foreign Secretary find it tolerable for major debates in his sphere of responsibility to take place in an assembly of which he was not a member. Accordingly, Lord Salisbury was passed over and Harold Macmillan went to the Foreign Office. Sir Anthony's opinion has been supported by Lord Strang, an ex-Permanent Under-Secretary at the Foreign Office, who also thought it would be impossible to have a Foreign Secretary in the Lords.[3]

A few months after the publication of Sir Anthony's book, Harold Macmillan, now Prime Minister, chose Lord Home as Foreign Secretary, and another Cabinet member, Edward Heath the Lord Privy Seal, was nominated as Foreign Office spokesman in the Commons. This led to another Opposition protest in the Commons, much sharper and more acrimonious in tone than the parallel debate in 1938. On this occasion the attack was not merely on a matter of constitutional principle but was linked

---

[1] H.C. Deb., Vol. 332, cols. 861–86.
[2] *Full Circle* (Cassell), pp. 273–4.
[3] *Home and Abroad* (Deutsch, 1956), p. 300.

with personal criticism of Lord Home.[1] Hugh Gaitskell, Leader of the Opposition, argued that

' . . . foreign affairs concern the lives and destinies of all of us today. They are not a subject about which it is the prerogative or privilege of a few people to argue. They are something which concern the whole of our people, indeed, the whole of mankind. In our opinion it is essential for this reason that the Foreign Secretary should be in the House of Commons so that, through the elected Members of the House of Commons, he can be in constant touch with public opinion and so that he can be here in this Chamber exposed to criticism and questioning.'[2]

The Prime Minister's defence was that Lord Home was the best man for the job and that Sir Anthony's point about adequate representation in the Commons was covered by the appointment of a second Foreign Office minister with a seat in the Cabinet. He also noted that the Foreign Secretary was able to give but limited attention to Parliament. 'In the last year the Foreign Secretary was absent on business from this country for 125 days, 75 of them while Parliament was sitting. He was able to answer Oral Questions on only 5 of the 24 Foreign Office days.'[3]

The 1960 pattern of ministerial appointments lasted for three years and caused no outstanding difficulties. Yet the circumstances were exceptional. Both the major controversial initiatives during this period, the decision to apply for membership of the European Common Market and the Nassau Agreement, were in a peculiar degree the personal responsibility of the Prime Minister, while the detailed Common Market negotiations were in the charge of Edward Heath, the Foreign Office spokesman in the Commons. The major international crisis, Cuba, came to a head when Parliament was in recess and so was not debated. That the arrangement worked adequately does not constitute justification. It can well be argued that Lord Home's nomination flaunted the democratic process and implied an unhealthy contempt for the House of Commons. A Foreign

[1] H. C.Deb., Vol. 627, cols. 1973–2006. The Opposition case received some support from an independent-minded Government backbencher, Gerald Nabarro.
[2] *Ibid.*, col. 1974.   [3] *Ibid*, col. 1996.

Secretary should not be arbitrarily divorced from the tides of opinion that surge through the Commons: the most remarkable feature of Halifax's unwavering support for the appeasement of Nazi Germany was his utter incomprehension of the widespread and growing revulsion for this policy.[1] In 1960–3 the relative absence of difficulty was not due to the lack of effective discussion in the Commons; rather was it due to the dominant role that the Prime Minister now plays in foreign affairs, making the Foreign Secretaryship less important. It is significant that no-one since Sir Anthony Eden has improved his political stature while holding the Foreign Secretaryship—with the possible exception of Lord Home.

The Commons were again deprived of a Foreign Secretary from October, 1964, to January, 1965, because Labour's Shadow minister and nominee for the post, Patrick Gordon Walker, was defeated at the General Election and a vacancy was created so that he might return to the House at a by-election. However, at the historic Leyton by-election he was again defeated. In view of past history it was impossible for a Labour Prime Minister to circumvent the difficulty by sending his Foreign Secretary to the Lords. Another immediate by-election in a safer seat than Leyton was judged to be an impossible embarrassment. Thus Gordon Walker's resignation was inevitable. Again, the three month absence of the Foreign Secretary from the Commons caused no real difficulty. The Prime Minister, Harold Wilson, made the major policy statements and speeches on foreign policy; other parliamentary business was dealt with by non-Cabinet Foreign Office ministers.

Can we expect, in future, that the Foreign Secretary will be a member of the Commons? He certainly will be under a Labour Government. With the Conservatives, the answer is unclear. A new situation has been created by the Peerage Act, 1963, which permits heirs to hereditary titles to renounce their rights at the time of succession. If it becomes usual for Conservative Members in this position to renounce their peerages, then it seems increasingly unlikely that any Conservative peer would have sufficient authority in the Party and the country to be offered the post of Foreign Secretary.

[1] Francis Williams, *A Pattern of Rulers* (Longmans, 1965), pp. 245–8.

GENERAL DEBATES

We now turn from Ministers to Members and examine the types of occasion when foreign affairs can be considered by the Commons. Major debates on foreign affairs occupy one or two full days. They have several procedural origins. First, at least in chronological terms, is the debate on the Address in reply to the Queen's Speech. Each session opens with the Gracious Speech from the Throne which announces, in outline, Cabinet policy for the coming year. The first important business in both Houses is discussion of this Speech, allowing a wide-ranging examination of Government policy that lasts usually five days. One of these days is devoted to the international situation and so there is always a foreign affairs debate early in each session. Other major debates in government time may be held on a motion approving specific aspects of Cabinet policy; on August 3, 1961, the Commons agreed to such a motion supporting the decision to re-open negotiations to join the European Common Market. Alternatively, the motion 'that this House do now adjourn' can be used as a procedural peg for a major debate that, by agreement between the parties, is limited to foreign affairs. This device has the advantage that discourse is not fettered by any need to be relevant to the wording of a reasoned motion and the argument can develop freely. The famous debate in May, 1940, that led to the fall of the Chamberlain Government is an example of the use of the adjournment motion to stage parliamentary business of the highest importance.

Through a Vote of Censure the Opposition can force a debate on any subject at any time but, by convention, the right is utilized only once or twice a session. In addition, there are the Supply Days when the Opposition decides the topic for debate. In terms of procedure, Supply Days have two forms. The Opposition can choose one or more of the annual estimates of expenditure for examination, and if it were desired to discuss foreign policy the Opposition would select the Votes of money for the Foreign Office. Or—and this technique is increasingly popular—the Opposition can put down certain Votes for review, agree to them without any debate, and then use the time saved to propose either a reasoned motion critical of Government policy or an adjournment motion. Supply Days are not norm-

74

ally used on world affairs; instead they become attacks on the Government's handling of economic and social problems because domestic topics provide better chances to stimulate popular dissatisfaction with Ministers.[1] However, a major two-day debate on foreign policy can be arranged through the Opposition offer of a Supply Day combined with a day from Government time.[2] Another form of horse trading through the usual channels works broadly on these lines. The Government propose to spend a day on, say, the second reading of a Bill: if the Bill is non-contentious the Opposition may see no advantage in discussing it at such length, so they suggest that the second reading is agreed about 7 p.m., instead of the usual 10 p.m., so that three hours can be devoted to something else that the Opposition feels to be of greater import.

Frequency of major foreign affairs debates varies very considerably. If the international scene is tense and causes a deep division of opinion between the parties, arguments thereon will be frequent and heated. The Suez crisis of 1956 is an obvious example of this situation. If the international scene is relatively peaceful and the main parties are generally agreed in their attitudes, debates will be infrequent and harmonious as in the 1962–3 session described in detail in the following chapter. When there is a consensus between the front benches but a strong minority opinion in the Opposition party, the Opposition leaders may avoid pressing for a foreign affairs debate as it would serve mainly to parade the disunity in their own ranks. Such a position arose in the Labour Party during the 'Bevanite' controversy 1952–5. Ministers may try to avoid debate when faced with important international negotiations since they will wish to escape from making public declarations which could hamper subsequent freedom of action at the conference table. Nor do they wish to provide other governments with evidence of lack of support in Britain for their own policies. Should the attitude of the Cabinet be supported firmly by the Opposition, the contrary applies and parliamentary debate could strengthen

[1] Cf. Anthony Barker's study of Supply procedure in *Political Studies*, Vol. XIII, pp. 45–64. Unfortunately Barker's figures on the use of Supply time distinguish only between home and overseas affairs, but not between foreign, Commonwealth and colonial affairs.

[2] H.C. Deb., Vol. 714, col. 892.

the position of our negotiators. If the Government cannot elude its critics prior to vital international discussions, then official spokesmen will be careful to avoid any commitments. One example is the Supply Day used on the Nassau Agreement in November, 1964, when Prime Minister Wilson's speech was a masterly exercise in saying very little:[1] inevitably he was not prepared to prejudice his forthcoming talks with President Johnson.

Every Government is constantly under pressure to agree to hold debates on a wide variety of topics; since parliamentary time is limited, many of these demands must go unsatisfied. Business for the Commons in the coming week is announced after question-time on Thursday. It is after this statement that Members can ask the Government to arrange debates on matters of special concern to them, and this opportunity is used frequently by critics of foreign policy. Requests from back-benchers can usually be brushed aside but those from Opposition leaders require careful consideration. It has been noted already that the Opposition can force discussion of any topic if determined to do so; thus it is in the interest of the Government to co-operate with the Opposition by trying to arrange a programme of business that is mutually acceptable. This can mean holding debates on international affairs on dates that fit in conveniently with missions abroad by the Foreign Secretary.

The timetable of major debates is determined by fairly rigid conventions. Normally they commence at, or soon after, 3.30 p.m. and conclude at 10 p.m. Opening and closing speeches each day are made from Government and Opposition front benches, the initial contributions occupy approximately forty-five minutes each, and the winding-up starts at 9 p.m. allowing half-an-hour for both sides. It follows that about four hours remain for backbenchers, including one speech from a Liberal M.P. As backbenchers normally speak for roughly twenty minutes, about ten of them will catch the Speaker's eye in a one-day debate or twenty in two days.

Major speeches are, of course, made by the Foreign Secretary and his opposite number in the Shadow Cabinet. The Prime Minister and the Leader of the Opposition may participate if they judge the debate to be of sufficient importance. Otherwise

[1] H.C. Deb., Vol. 702, cols. 930–48.

the Foreign Secretary will usually be supported by a Minister of State from his own Department. In a two-day debate, which requires four front-bench contributors, assistance will come from other members of the Cabinet and the Opposition will put forward more of their leading personalities. The Labour and Conservative front benches tend to nominate pairs of speakers of broadly similar status in the respective party hierarchies. Back-benchers have to catch Mr. Speaker's eye. A Member who wishes to enter a debate informs his Whip, who passes the information through the Whips' office to the Speaker; alterna-tively a Member can communicate with the Speaker directly. Often far more Members wish to speak than can be fitted in to the time available. According to Emrys Hughes (Lab. South Ayrshire)[1] over eighty Members wished to join in the last foreign affairs debate of 1965: inevitably four-fifths of them were disappointed. Traditionally the task of the Chair is to produce a varied and balanced debate. Contributions generally come from alternate sides of the Chamber. Members with unorthodox or extreme views have an above-average chance of being heard. Backbenchers tend to specialise on particular subjects and those who join in debates on foreign affairs will also be active in the unofficial party committees dealing with this field.[2] Certain Members appear fairly regularly in *Hansard* when the Commons are reviewing international problems, but it would be wrong to infer that these debates are dominated by a limited clique. There is no other subject which attracts so much detailed interest and concern.

The tone of debate is greatly affected by whether it is expected to end with a challenge to the Government in the division lobbies. If a vote is not anticipated, a variety of opinion will emerge yet contributions are likely to be constructive; if it is, then much energy will be spent on political partisanship, loyalty will predominate and fewer intra-party fissures will appear.

Attendance at debates fluctuates widely. At moments of crisis a major speech from the Prime Minister will see the Chamber crammed beyond capacity, and there is usually a good audience for the opening front-bench contributions. But when the time comes for backbenchers, Members tend to move

[1] *Parliament and Mumbo-Jumbo*, (Allen & Unwin, 1966), p. 110.
[2] The work of these bodies is discussed on pp. 133-7 *infra*.

away from the Chamber to attend to their correspondence or other business, or merely to seek refreshment and informal conversation. The Minister due to reply to a debate is expected to attend the greater part of the preceding discussion, the Opposition front bench should always have at least one occupant, a few whips hover around, but otherwise the undistinguished backbencher may find that he is addressing only a handful of Members, many of whom are awaiting a chance to speak themselves. In the main communal rooms for Members in the Palace of Westminster there are silent annunciators showing the name of the Member speaking in the Chamber, and this enables the House to assemble rapidly if it is thought that an important speech is being made. Then the Chamber tends to fill again about 9 p.m. as Members arrive to hear the end of the debate, and attendance at this time is greatly increased if the proceedings are to terminate with a division at 10 p.m. However, since the major parties are generally broadly agreed on basic issues of foreign policy, these debates frequently end without a vote being challenged.

Critics of Parliament often comment unfavourably about the sparse attendance of Members in the Chamber. Yet even if those present are few, the potential audience is vast. Any little-known backbencher can command the attention of Press, radio and television reporters if he makes a sufficiently striking or well-informed speech. If he shows mastery of international affairs he will enhance his reputation not only with party leaders, but also in diplomatic circles and with professional students of foreign policy.

LEGISLATION

Foreign affairs is a matter for negotiation rather than legislation, and in negotiations international law is of greater import than the domestic law of the homeland. Thus Foreign Office Ministers spend less time steering Bills through Parliament than do the Ministers of other major Departments. Indeed, much of the legislation which is a direct consequence of international agreements ceases, at the stage of parliamentary consideration, to be the responsibility of the Foreign Office.

The extent to which parliamentary action is required, or is possible, in connexion with treaty ratification was examined above. It was shown that some treaties and agreements are not fully effective without a change in British law. This is because British Courts base their decisions on British law and will not accept the authority of international agreements made by the British Government. An excellent example of this principle is provided by the litigation arising from the disposition of the estate of the deceased ex-King of Italy.[1] Under the terms of a financial agreement made in 1947 between the British and Italian Governments these assets could have become available to the Italian Government for the purpose of paying debts in the United Kingdom. However, this agreement was not effective since no action had been taken to give it legislative effect, and the judge held that 'the Financial Agreement is not recognizable or justiciable in this Court.' Where possible a British Court will construe Acts of Parliament so that they do not conflict with international law, but where conflict is inescapable the British law must be obeyed.[2] The position under international law is different. The Permanent Court of International Justice has held repeatedly that a state cannot obtain justification for avoiding its international obligations by reference to its own internal legislation.[3] It follows that there is a moral obligation on any government to ensure that its domestic legislation does not impede the fulfilment of international agreements, except in the case of an agreement which is made subject to the condition of subsequent parliamentary approval. This obligation is most fully accepted in the Netherlands where, in the case of conflict between international agreements and domestic law, precedence is accorded to later-created international commitments.[4]

The following list of some recent British statutes necessitated by international agreements illustrates the wide variety of this type of legislation.

European Free Trade Association Act, 1960. To apply the convention establishing E.F.T.A. to British law. Departmental responsibility: Board of Trade.

[1] *The Republic of Italy v. Hambros Bank Ltd., and Gregory (Custodian of Enemy Property)* [1950], Ch. 314.
[2] T. E. Holland, *Studies in International Law* (O.U.P., 1898), p. 199.
[3] Lord McNair, *Law of Treaties* (O.U.P., 1961), pp. 757–62.
[4] Buck and Travis (eds.), *Control of Foreign Relations in Modern Nations* (Norton, 1957), pp. 588–9.

Parliament and Foreign Affairs

Carriage by Air Act, 1961. To apply to this country the Hague Protocol, 1955, increasing the liability of air carriers for death or injury to passengers or damage to goods. A private member's Bill sponsored by Ronald Bell (Con. South Buckinghamshire).

South Africa Act, 1962. To provide for the legal consequences of the decision that South Africa should leave the Commonwealth. Departmental responsibility: Foreign Office.

Civil Aviation (Eurocontrol) Act, 1962. To authorise participation in the European Organisation for the Safety of Air Navigation, an organisation which arose out of an Agreement between the United Kingdom, France, Belgium, Holland, Luxembourg and West Germany. Departmental responsibility: Ministry of Aviation.

International Monetary Fund Act, 1962. To authorise United Kingdom participation in the IMF scheme to enable it to acquire additional resources. Departmental responsibility: Treasury.

Continental Shelf Act, 1964. The result of the Conference on the Law of the Sea at Geneva in 1958 which was followed by the British signatures to the Continental Shelf Convention and the High Seas Convention. The Act provides the legal basis for exploration for and exploitation of underwater oil in the North Sea. Departmental responsibility: Ministry of Power.

Diplomatic Privileges Act, 1964. To give effect to the Vienna Convention of Diplomatic Relations relating to legal immunities and privileges and to authorize ratification of the Convention. Departmental responsibility: Foreign Office.

Fishery Limits Act, 1964. To apply the conditions of the Fisheries Convention of 1964 to British coastal waters and thus free our inshore fishermen from foreign interference over a wider area. Departmental responsibility: Ministry of Agriculture.

None of these Acts created major political controversy. In no case was a division challenged on the second reading, and their passage to the Statute Book was relatively smooth and uncomplicated. Should it be more convenient, measures of this type may be introduced in the Lords and then passed on to the Commons. Only two of the eight Acts noted above came under the aegis of the Foreign Office. The Act dealing with diplomatic immunities aroused the greatest concern in the Commons where some supporters of the Conservative Government feared that espionage might be facilitated. The Carriage by Air Act is something of an oddity since the use of private member's time to authorize participation in international agreements is unusual. Had this country joined the European Common Market in 1963 the consequent legislation would, of course, have been controversial and of unique complexity.

Any measure to implement an international agreement creates a difficulty in the sense that it is usually necessary to accept it *in toto* since any amendment would almost certainly be contrary to the terms of the arrangements already accepted by the Government. So if either House of Parliament passes an amendment to such a Bill, the effect is to demand a re-negotiation of the original agreement. A move of this kind would place Ministers in a position of grave embarrassment. Due to the strength of party loyalty this eventuality is unlikely to occur in the modern Parliament, but Ministers may be tempted to defend the details of this type of legislation not on its merits, but on the basis that Parliament must accept international engagements as a whole, since it becomes diplomatically impossible to reject limited sections of an international agreement. A similar situation arises with internal legislation—admittedly in a less acute form—when the details of a Bill represent the result of negotiations between Ministers and influential interested parties: here again the outcome of parliamentary debate must be prejudged if the Government cannot modify proposed legislation without defaulting on prior commitments.

Not every parliamentary Bill that concerns the Foreign Office is the consequence of diplomatic activity, e.g. the Foreign Service Act, 1960, a brief uncontroversial measure relating to the payment of pensions to those officials who leave the Foreign Service before the normal retiring age. Also in this category would fall the Foreign Compensation Act, 1962, which is described in more detail below in the detailed case-study of the session 1962–3.

Statutory Instruments, the Orders issued by Ministers under the authority of previous legislation, can also have relevance to international affairs. Discussions on Orders are usually short, and arouse no interest. Two types of procedure are used. Some Orders require a confirmatory resolution in both Houses to come into effect and must therefore be subject to debate: others become law immediately on publication, or after a specified period, and are discussed in Parliament only if they arouse objections and a 'prayer' for amendment is moved. Orders total two thousand or more a year, but few are the responsibility of the Foreign Office and of these but a small proportion are debated. Their subject-matter is narrow and technical; common subjects for Foreign Office Orders are diplomatic immunities and privileges and questions of foreign compensation. Parliamentary procedure requires that all Statutory Instruments must be accepted or rejected as a whole; unlike Bills, they cannot be amended. This must damage the ability of Parliament to exert control in this field and the contents of an Order can be influenced only by pressure that is exerted before the date of publication.[1]

QUESTIONS

The first recorded parliamentary question was connected with foreign affairs. In January, 1721, Robert Knight, chief cashier of the corrupt South Sea Company absconded but was subsequently arrested in Brussels. On February 9th, Earl Cowper asked a question in the Lords designed to confirm the information of Knight's arrest. The Parliamentary History[2] records that 'the Earl of Sutherland having upon this informed the House in what manner Mr Knight had been apprehended and secured, a motion was made to address His Majesty to order his ministers abroad to use the most effectual instances to have him delivered up and sent over.' This was not easily arranged for the request for extradition had to be communicated to the Emperor in Vienna. The significance of this event was the institution of a new form of parliamentary proceeding for Earl Cowper was not speaking to a motion, the traditional basis of all parliamentary discourse; instead, he was simply asking the Government for information. But it was another half-century before questions began to constitute a significant aspect of parliamentary proceedings: largely this was due to the political quiescence during the period of Whig supremacy. In 1792 the importance of questions was powerfully reinforced when the Duke of Leeds resigned office as Foreign Secretary, admitting his fault in failing to answer questions about British intervention in the war

[1] For an example, the Foreign Compensation (Egypt) Order 1963, see below p. 113.
[2] Vol. 7, col. 709.

between Prussia, Turkey and Russia. Questions were often answered in the earlier part of the nineteenth century with what today would be regarded as appalling frankness. The ignorance of the Government about developments abroad was revealed. Answers given on the conduct of the Crimea War not only demonstrated official incompetence but were answered in detail which showed utter disregard for military security.[1] Subsequently, greater caution prevailed.

The development of supplementary questions has slowly changed the character of question-time, because the additional questions and answers are—to some degree—unpredictable and introduce an element of potential drama in the question period. Originally, the practice of allowing supplementaries caused misgiving but the Speaker of the Commons felt impelled to allow additional interrogation if a ministerial answer was inadequate or unsatisfactory. Then the right to ask a supplementary extended from the original questioner to any other Member who felt dissatisfied with a ministerial answer. According to Sir Charles Dilke the practice of asking supplementary questions on foreign affairs commenced in 1882.[2] An unguarded, spontaneous reply on a matter of foreign policy could clearly produce an awkward situation for the Government. The prospect was aggravated because at this period the Foreign Secretary was always in the House of Lords,[3] so Commons' questions on foreign affairs were normally dealt with by a junior minister. Fear of unguarded statements led to a Government decision in 1899 that the Under-Secretary of State for Foreign Affairs would not answer supplementary questions. Two years later this ruling was challenged by an emergency adjournment debate, and the Leader of the House, Mr Balfour, defended the refusal to answer supplementaries by arguing 'it is impossible, if such a practice is to prevail, to carry on the difficult and delicate negotiations in which an Empire of this magnitude is constantly involved'. At a division the motion to adjourn was rejected, and Government policy was approved, by a majority of forty-

[1] P. Howarth, *Questions in the House*, (Bodley Head, 1956), p. 136 *et seq.*
[2] Parl. Deb., (1901), 4th series, Vol. 89, col. 340. At this period the reports of parliamentary debates were not a verbatim record, and supplementary questions and answers were commonly excluded.
[3] See p. 69 *supra.*

five[1]. When the Liberals returned to power in 1906 the ban on supplementaries disappeared. But this short-lived restriction has a double significance. It shows that foreign affairs were regarded as being in a special category of their own: there was no corresponding ban on questions on Colonial matters for no other Governments were involved. Secondly, it indicated a singular lack of Cabinet confidence in the discretion of a minister under fire at question-time.

The rise in the number of questions asked and the evolution of supplementaries led inevitably to the need to limit the time made available for this sector of parliamentary activity. In 1902 a limit of forty minutes was introduced. Four years later the new Liberal Government extended the period to an hour, minus a few minutes for prayers and items of private business, and this is the position today. Another change initiated in 1902 was the grouping together on the Order Paper of questions addressed to the same Minister. When this system started it was organized essentially to meet ministerial convenience: the priority allocated to Departments was not a matter of major importance since forty minutes was usually adequate to deal with all questions. Subsequently the time allowed became increasingly inadequate and the questions not reached by the end of the question period were either given a written answer recorded in *Hansard* or had to be withdrawn and put down for oral answer on a later day. In these circumstances, their priority on the Order Paper was of general concern. A rota of Departments was arranged for each of the four days Monday to Thursday when business opened with the question period. The rota has been subject to many changes and has become increasingly complicated.[2] As far as foreign affairs are concerned, the cumulative effect of successive changes has been to reduce substantially their priority at question-time. In 1914 Foreign Office questions were taken first on Mondays, Tuesdays and Thursdays: ten years later they were first on Wednesdays and third on Mondays: in 1929 they became first on Wednesdays and second on Mondays. Since

[1] Parl. Deb. 4th series, Vol. 89, cols. 322–68. This discussion is a good example of the relative ease with which an emergency adjournment debate could be obtained. In this instance the 'urgent matter of public importance' under consideration was a Government policy already two years old!

[2] For full details see D. N. Chester and Nona Bowring, *Questions in Parliament* (O.U.P., 1962), Ch. 6.

1945 the rota has been spread over a number of weeks: six or seven Ministries were due for questions each day, but the week after coming top of the list a ministry dropped to the bottom. This was done to ensure that each Department had a turn at the head of the daily queue of questions. Thus the Foreign Office lost its absolute precedence each Wednesday. Instead it was placed in a seven-week rota on Mondays and Wednesdays, so that it came top of the list approximately once every three-and-a-half weeks. Some other Departments, e.g. the Treasury, Agriculture and Housing and Local Government, were similarly treated, but most Departments appeared on the rota only on one day each week. In January, 1964, these arrangements were changed so that every Department is now included only on a single day each week. This has the advantage that the length of the rota could be shortened and each Department has first turn a little more frequently—save, of course, the few Departments including the Foreign Office which previously had enjoyed (or suffered) a double ration. A further advantage is that Ministers from the former 'double ration' Departments are now liable to be tied to the House at question-time for one day a week instead of two: a Minister must be present to answer even if it be certain that the question period will expire before his questions are reached. Such is the pressure now that it is quite common for the whole of the time available to be occupied by the Department that heads the daily list; as many as five parliamentary weeks may pass without an opportunity arising of putting oral questions to a Foreign Office spokesman.

It is true that there are other opportunities to ask questions on foreign policy. Should an M.P. merely require information he can put down an unstarred question for written reply on any day from Monday to Friday when Parliament is sitting. Urgent matters of great importance can be raised through the private notice procedure, but this technique is used sparingly and depends on the permission of the Speaker. In addition, the Prime Minister answers questions from 3.15 to 3.30 p.m. on Tuesdays and Thursdays: these questions often raise major issues of foreign policy. A Prime Minister can decide whether to answer questions addressed to him or have them transferred to other Ministers. However, all Prime Ministers normally reply to questions concerning discussions with or representations to or from other Heads of Government. Certain types of question must be accepted by the Prime Minister, for example those arising from his journeys abroad, those about departmental co-ordination and those which involve the responsibility of more than one Minister—questions concerning disarmament or NATO defence talks bring in the Foreign Office and the Ministry of Defence. Further, a Prime Minister is normally willing to answer on matters of major importance and on problems which have attracted his personal interest. Macmillan took questions about nuclear bomb testing and test-ban treaties and, at one stage, major Common Market questions; Wilson is answering on Vietnam. The involvement of the Prime Minister is also increased by the skill of Members in framing questions in such a way that he cannot easily transfer them. So although the practice varies from time to time, the Prime Minister deals with a number of foreign questions in his quarter-hour periods on Tuesday and Thursday, and these may raise specific, and even narrow issues, which in other branches of Government business would fall naturally to the Departmental Minister.

Even so, compared with their absolute priority three days a week in 1914, there has been a dramatic reduction in the status of foreign policy questions. Does the change imply that Members regard them as less significant or less suitable for parliamentary investigation than they did half a century ago? Of course not. But a new situation has arisen in that Members are more deeply involved in the problems of their constituencies. Far more purely local issues are raised at question-time. Far more supplementaries are asked and progress is slowed down. All this has come from the growth of state concern with economic and social welfare, the rise in parliamentary salaries and the extra demands by constituents on the time and energy of their Members. Under these pressures foreign affairs have had to surrender precedence at question-time.

All parliamentary questions are restricted by the rules of order which govern what questions may be asked, or how they may be worded. A few of the rules have important implications for foreign affairs. In particular, any matter raised must fall within the responsibility of Ministers. Thus if there should be an attempted revolution in Ruritania, no question could be asked directly about the cause of the uprising. Any attempt to

raise the internal problems of Ruritania at question-time can
only succeed if the question is worded so as to enquire whether
the British Government had made any representations to that
country on a particular matter or, more generally, whether
recent events in Ruritainia have affected relations between that
country and ours. Another rule is that a question must not
refer discourteously to a friendly foreign country.

Foreign affairs tend to be raised by a few Members on both
sides of the House who specialise in this subject. Their questions
are almost wholly political; they act as opening gambits for a
challenge to government policy in the form of a brief interrogation through supplementary questions. Naturally this is well
understood by Ministers and their civil service advisers, so the
intent behind the question affects the type of reply offered.
Often this will be brief and framed in such a way as to limit,
as far as possible, the scope for supplementaries. The Minister
and his advisers will anticipate, usually with great accuracy,
the supplementaries that follow. Ministerial responses are well
prepared. Much forethought is given to this work: we have
moved far from the days when Balfour feared for the consequences of an ill-considered reply. The Minister has a substantial
advantage in the cut and thrust of question and answer. He is
backed by the resources of his Department: he is helped also by
the pattern of procedure which limits the number of supplementary questions on each topic, and which allows a Member on
the Government benches to side-track the Opposition attack by
putting a supplementary which confuses the issue. It is rare for a
backbencher to be able to score points effectively against a
Minister.

These general considerations apply with particular force to
foreign affairs. Here the political element must be dominant,
for, as compared with home departments, the questions will not
refer to constituency problems and only rarely to an individual
grievance. There are a few references to the Foreign Service,
but the majority of questions imply no challenge to the daily
routine of the Foreign Office. This concentration on political
policy means that Foreign Office questions tend not to invoke
the concept of ministerial responsibility for details of departmental administration.

However, a variety of useful purposes are achieved by

parliamentary interrogation. It may enable a statement to be made showing the Government view of a changing situation or a new problem; the regular publicity for parliamentary proceedings in the Press and on radio and television ensures that such a policy statement will become widely known. It also keeps Ministers in touch with public opinion and provides an opportunity for critics to challenge any aspect of foreign policy.[1] Inevitably, most of the criticism comes from the Opposition, but a Government may also encounter hostile fire from its own backbenchers: some left-wing Labour Members now use question-time as a means to urge the Government to disassociate itself from United States policy in Vietnam. Thus the channel of communication provided is essentially that of a two-way flow. Finally, a question may act as a catalyst and force the Government to frame a policy after a period of hesitation and doubt. A major example of this nature is the 1939 guarantee to Poland of British aid in the event of any attack on her independence, a guarantee that was improvised in reply to a parliamentary question asking what action the Government would take in the event of a German attack on Poland.[2]

MOTION FOR THE ADJOURNMENT

The motion for the adjournment is used for several types of debate. It is highly convenient because it allows speeches to range widely, unrestricted by the terms of a reasoned motion. The Government may arrange that the main business of the day shall take the form of a discussion on the question 'that the House do now adjourn'—in relation to foreign affairs this is peculiarly suitable when the Opposition does not wish to make a specific challenge to ministerial policy.

Under Standing Order No. 9, the motion for the adjournment may also be used in an emergency to raise a matter of public importance, although there are many procedural difficulties in the way of obtaining such a debate. At the end of questions a Member can move the adjournment of the House to discuss

---

[1] The value of question-time has been stressed by Kenneth Younger, a former junior minister at the Foreign Office, in *The British Journal of Sociology* (1955), Vol. VI, pp. 172–3, in his article 'Public Opinion and Foreign Policy'.

[2] Lord Strang, *Home and Abroad* (Deutsch, 1956), p. 161.

some recent development; the Speaker will not accept the motion unless the subject is specific, urgent, of sufficient gravity, falls within the responsibility of Ministers and there is no other opportunity in the near future to consider it. If the Speaker accepts the motion, and forty Members support it, the main business of the day is interrupted at 7 p.m. for the emergency debate. The delay until 7 p.m. gives all concerned time to prepare for the discussion, which normally causes much excitement. Requests for an emergency adjournment come usually from the Opposition, but an overwhelming majority fail to meet the severe requirements. Rulings from the Chair about Standing Order 9 have become increasingly restrictive during this century, and especially so since the election of Speaker Whitley in 1921. This has damaged seriously the ability of backbenchers to initiate immediate discussion on serious incidents in home, foreign or colonial affairs. Whether an incident is of sufficient gravity, and whether there is a reasonable alternative opportunity for raising it in the near future are matters of opinion, but the Speaker is bound by precedent to interpret the procedural requirements strictly. Accordingly in February, 1966, the Speaker, Dr King, had to refuse an emergency debate on the resumption of bombing in North Vietnam by the United States, but the tone of his ruling seemed to imply sympathy with the request.[1]

Between 1939 and 1958 only ten out of 103 attempts to claim an emergency adjournment were successful: nineteen of these occasions related to foreign affairs and only one was successful, while five out of twenty-five attempts connected with colonial matters succeeded.[2] The sole foreign affairs debate in this category took place in 1946 over the British evacuation of Egypt and was requested by Churchill, then Leader of the Opposition.[3]

The virtual disuse of this procedure has led to various suggestions designed to increase its availability. Several proposals of this nature were put forward by the 1959 Select Committee on Procedure, but none of them was accepted by the Govern-

[1] H.C. Deb., Vol. 723, cols. 886–9.
[2] W. H. Greenleaf, 'Urgency Motions in the Commons' in *Public Law*, 1960, pp. 277 and 280.
[3] H.C. Deb., Vol. 422, cols. 781–4 and 849–906.

ment.[1] One of the Committee's suggestions had special reference to foreign affairs: it was that 'motions about foreign affairs in which no Government responsibility is immediately involved should nonetheless be in order if it seems that the Government might subsequently be concerned'. This, surely, would be a most reasonable relaxation of the rules. Any major diplomatic crisis today concerns the whole world. It may speedily become the subject of discussion at the United Nations in which a British representative will participate. British policy should not be made known at an international forum prior to debate in the House of Commons merely because of a procedural technicality. There may, of course, be difficulties if a Minister is required to make a considered statement to the House about a crisis abroad at three hours' notice. But a Government spokesman, if he must, can always stonewall.

The third use of the adjournment motion is to permit short debates initiated by backbenchers. Half an hour at the end of business each day is allowed for this purpose, together with the whole of the last day of the session and the days immediately prior to adjournment for the Christmas, Easter, Whitsun and summer recesses. Allocation of the half-hour adjournment is decided by ballot, except on Thursdays. Subjects for Thursday evenings and the holiday adjournments are chosen by the Speaker from suggestions received from Members on the understanding that he will give priority to topical matters and urgent constituency grievances. Again, there is a bar against raising issues for which the Government has no responsibility. Foreign affairs rarely enter into the daily half-hour discussions. They do sometimes arise at the holiday adjournments when a number of topics are raised on a timetable fixed by the Speaker in which more than half an hour is allowed for the more important items.

MINISTERIAL STATEMENTS

Explanations of ministerial policy can be made to the Commons after questions, with minor statements at morning sittings. This procedure is especially useful as it enables the Government to give the House its views of the latest developments in any international issues which affect British interests. Such statements can be made in reply to a private notice question that has

[1] 1958–9 (92) vi. para. 34 and H.C. Deb., Vol. 617, cols. 150–4.

been pre-arranged with the Minister: a private notice question may be asked only with the permission of the Speaker, it does not require the normal 48 hours notice and it must refer to a topic of some urgency.[1] But many statements now dispense with any such prelude. Prior notice of them must be given to the Speaker, although permission of the House is not required. When a statement has been made there is, in terms of the technicalities of parliamentary procedure, no 'question' before the House to discuss and so any debate would be irregular. However, this rule is applied with a little flexibility. A ministerial pronouncement is commonly followed by questions and, if the matter is of great importance, the leaders of opposition parties may make comments. This can produce something of a minature debate until the Chair insists that the House returns to the main business of the day. It is, of course, possible for a ministerial statement to be made and debated on the motion for the adjournment: Wilson's announcement of the projected Commonwealth peace mission on Vietnam was made on the half-hour adjournment debate, the Member who had previously been allocated the adjournment having relinquished his right to use it.[2] To use the half-hour adjournment in this fashion is most exceptional.

The fact that major policy developments are announced in Parliament ensures that it remains an important channel of communication between Government and the Public. Opposition spokesmen frequently protest if, when the House is in session, intimations of official policy are made available for the Press and broadcasting authorities prior to any statement to Parliament. Some of the 'leaks' of information that occur may be accidental; some, quite obviously, are not. In future, Parliament may become less compelling as an arena that ensures publicity, for Ministers know they can make a much greater public impact by appearing on television than by speaking at

[1] A Minister may also ask leave at the end of question-time to reply to a question on the Order Paper that was not reached before the question-hour expired. Strictly speaking, this is an exceptional extension of the question period rather than a ministerial statement. But the effect is similar in that it allows a Minister to speak on a matter of topical importance that could not otherwise have been raised.

[2] H.C. Deb., Vol. 714, col. 1046.

Westminster. There is also difficulty about interrupting Commons' debates, and the rigidity of procedure introduces unnecessary impediments to the announcement of new policies. Thus on June 17, 1965, it seems that Harold Wilson wished to make his statement on the Vietnam peace mission about 8 p.m.:[1] had the adjournment of the House been moved to permit this, the proceedings on the Highlands and Islands Development Bill would have terminated and the final stages of the Bill could not have been completed that day. The reason for this complication is simple. If the main business of the day is interrupted by an adjournment motion, it cannot afterwards be resumed. As it was, the House kept the Prime Minister waiting until after 11 p.m. and in the meantime he appeared on the BBC *Gallery* programme to discuss the projected peace mission. This incident demonstrates clearly that the Commons must modify its procedure to facilitate Government statements if it wishes to be kept fully informed in moments of tension and if it wishes to retain any primacy as a source of news.

Members may also make personal statements to the Commons on matters concerning their personal integrity and on serious cases of misreporting and misinterpretation. In rare cases this could involve foreign affairs, for example if a Minister wished to clarify a statement that had been misunderstood abroad.[2] A Minister who resigns from the Cabinet due to major policy disagreement with his colleagues may also make an explanation to Parliament. Such occasions are highly infrequent because ministerial resignations on policy issues are uncommon and even when one occurs the right to make a statement is not always utilized: the last major resignation statements concerned with foreign affairs were in 1938.[3] Explanations of this type are not debatable; the tradition is for the House to listen in silence and sympathy and then pass on to its pre-arranged business, which may or may not be concerned with the subject of the

[1] Cf. Emanuel Shinwell's intervention, *ibid* col. 797.

[2] H.C. Deb., Vol. 680, cols. 337–41 (Heath): H.C. Deb., Vol. 730, cols. 1237–8 (Healey).

[3] H.C. Deb., Vol. 332, cols. 45–52 (Eden and Viscount Cranborne) and Vol. 339, cols. 29–40 (Duff Cooper). Christopher Mayhew (Lab. E. Woolwich) resigned on defence and foreign policy issues in 1966 but, as Minister of Defence for the Navy, he was not a member of the Cabinet. Vol. 725, cols. 254–65.

resignation. Of course, resignation statements may be the subject of comment in later debates.

There are some minor, miscellaneous items in the timetable of the Commons which give added flexibility to its proceedings and which may provide additional opportunities for the discussion of foreign affairs.

Each session Parliament is asked to agree to two or three Consolidated Fund Bills which authorise the issue of money from the Consolidated Fund to be spent on the business of government. The passage of these Bills is uncontentious in the sense that everyone agrees that the Crown must be provided with the money needed to honour its financial obligations. But they do provide a general opportunity for the discussion of ministerial policy and departmental administration. Two days are allocated to each of these Bills, one for the Second Reading the the other for the Committee Stage (which is a formality) and Third Reading. Each March and July one such Bill must be brought forward, and it is now usual for a third Bill to be required in December. The March and July Bills permit an unrestricted range of debate; discussion in December is limited to the subjects of the supplementary estimates covered by the Bill which, of course, may exclude foreign affairs. The choice of subject on these occasions is shared between the Opposition and the backbenchers. On two days a motion is moved from the Opposition front-bench and the debate ends at the usual time of ten o'clock. The remaining days are the backbenchers' opportunity and the outcome is similar to the series of discussions held on the day-long adjournment motion when the House goes into recess except that, as financial legislation is not subject to the automatic 10 o'clock closure, the proceedings may continue through the night.

When an important report has been published, the Government may be willing to provide time for a discussion of its conclusions. But often the Government refuses to arrange such a debate, either through shortage of parliamentary time or because it wishes to avoid detailed commitments in connexion with a report's recommendations. In this case the Opposition or a backbencher can force the issue to the extent of securing a debate: in July, 1964, a Government backbencher Humphry Berkeley (Con. Lancaster) used the Third Reading of the Consolidated Fund Bill to initiate a discussion[1] on the Plowden Committee Report[2] concerned with the future relationship of the Foreign Office and the Commonwealth Relations Office.

Consolidated Fund Bills and the estimates considered on Supply Days are Government business, although Ministers do not control the topics then debated. In private members' time the business belongs wholly to backbenchers: these periods are now limited to twenty Fridays and four other half days each session. Ten Fridays and the four half days are devoted to motions. Ten Fridays are devoted to Bills introduced by back-benchers. The right to initiate Bills or motions on these occasions is determined by ballot.[3] A Member may also introduce a Bill on Tuesdays or Wednesdays with a short ten-minute speech; a speech of similar length may be made in opposition and then the motion for leave to introduce the Bill is put. If this hurdle is surmounted the Bill goes into the queue of private members' Bills behind all those introduced on the ballot—and is thus almost certain never to appear again. As has been argued already, foreign affairs is a matter for negotiation rather than legislation so it would be rare for a private member's Bill to be concerned with international questions. A Member who did put forward such a Bill would do so not with any serious intention of proposing legislation but in order to propagate a particular viewpoint.

The motion procedure is obviously more suitable for the discussion of international problems. Yet, almost without exception, private members' motions relate to domestic issues— no doubt because it is thought that these produce the greatest dividends in terms of party advantage or constituency pop-ularity. This is well illustrated by the events of July 13, 1965, when a half-day was available for a backbench motion. As is customary, three names were drawn in the ballot and the successful Members informed the House a fortnight in advance of the topics they intended to discuss. First out of the hat, John

[1] H.C. Deb., Vol. 699, cols. 1456–88.

[2] 1963–4, Cmnd. 2276, xi.

[3] For a more detailed discussion of the use made of private members' time see Peter G. Richards: *Honourable Members* (Faber, 1964), Ch. 10.

Hall (Con. Wycombe), wished to talk about relations with Europe: second was Neil Marten (Con. Banbury) whose subject was the Campaign for Nuclear Disarmament. On these occasions it is virtually certain that all the time available will be spent on the first topic, and if any group of Members wish to avoid the second topic they can prolong discussion on the first until the end of the allotted time. Thus the motion on CND was unlikely to be reached. Conservatives felt, however, that the Government might be embarrassed by a debate on CND since it would enable emphasis to be put on the support previously given to this movement by some members of the Labour Cabinet. Hall withdrew his motion on Europe and political sniping about CND took its place.

Private members' time can make no major contribution to parliamentary discussion of foreign policy, but it can be of value if used to examine a specialized or secondary topic that is generally overlooked.

Finally, the Commons spend three days each session (and these include two of the Supply Days), in considering the reports of its financial committees, the Public Accounts Committee and the Estimates Committee. As their names imply these bodies examine respectively the accounts relating to past expenditure and the estimates of future spending. Three of the annual Votes of money concern the Foreign Office. One covers the Diplomatic Service which since 1965 has included the Commonwealth Service and the Trade Commission Service. The others deal with Foreign Services in general and the British Council.[1] Accounts of money spent under these headings are examined by the Comptroller and Auditor General who will report to the Public Accounts Committee if he finds evidence of waste or other cause for criticism. Foreign Office estimates may be examined by the Estimates Committee but any recommendations from this body must be consistent with the policies implied in the estimates. So the financial committees do not challenge Government policy; instead they try to ensure legality and economy in the use of public funds. It follows that they cannot be a forum for broad discussions on international prob-

[1] In 1966–7 anticipated expenditure was £38,259,000 on the Diplomatic Service, £18,693,000 on Foreign Services and £4,472,000 on the British Council: *Civil Estimates* Class II, 1965–6 (92).

lems and in recent years the Estimates Committee has made no major enquiry into the Foreign Office Votes.

THE HOUSE OF LORDS

Upholders of the House of Lords often argue that its debates are less political in tone than those in the Commons. This assertion is misleading. Their Lordships have political views and, quite inevitably, these colour the content of their speeches. But it is the case that the character of debates in the Lords is markedly different to the Commons. There is less desire to score political points; there is less interruption of speeches; there is almost no cut-and-thrust of debate to enliven the scene. The average age of the Lords is much higher and normally the atmosphere they engender is serene, undisturbed. From the Woolsack the Lord Chancellor presides over debates, but he has no disciplinary powers like those of the Speaker. Disorder is unknown: should the need arise to reprove a Noble Lord for not observing the conventions, the task would fall normally on the Leader of the House.

There are two chief methods of raising issues of foreign policy in the Lords, by question and by debate. Questions are many fewer than in the Commons; six is a usual number for one day. Ministerial answers are often fuller than in the lower House and the chairman has no authority to limit the length or number of supplementary questions. It follows that one question may occupy the House for several minutes and provoke a minor debate. Such flexibility is reminiscent of the House of Commons in the nineteenth century: it is extremely valuable but can be maintained solely in conditions of general placidity and low attendance.

Debates on foreign affairs can be initiated in a variety of ways. They are relatively easy to arrange since the Government does not dominate the time of the House except to some extent after Easter when a flow of legislation comes up from the Commons. Even at this period there is greater scope for adjustment and if a number of peers wished for a foreign policy discussion, it would be organised. Most Lords' debates are not opened by a Minister but by a peer moving a motion asking 'for papers', a procedural device that has no significance save that it gives the mover the right of reply to the debate. In addition, a debate may take place on a reasoned motion or arise out of a ministerial statement or an unstarred question. It is customary for one of the days spent discussing the Speech from the Throne to be devoted to foreign affairs. The tendency for foreign affairs to become interwoven with defence questions is even more marked than in the Commons, partly because of the wealth of military experience in the Upper House due to the practice of ennobling wartime commanders. A small group of peers give particular attention to foreign affairs and its members participate fairly regularly in debates thereon; prominent among them in recent years have been Lords Attlee, Carrington, Colyton, Gladwyn, Kennet, Rea, Salisbury, Taylor and Walston. Amongst their Lordships as a whole there is overwhelming majority support for the Conservative Party, but this is not always reflected in the pattern of debate when a substantial fraction of the time is occupied by Liberal or Labour sympathizers—one example of the general tendency for the Left-wing peers to be the more active members of the Upper House. A typical foreign affairs discussion runs from 3 p.m. until about 7.30 p.m. when the House adjourns for the day in time to dine. Usually a speech lasts about twenty minutes and the debate includes a dozen or fourteen contributions. The order of speaking is arranged beforehand but is not adhered to rigidly so that a peer may still contribute later in the debate should he not have been in the Chamber for his predetermined turn. If a large number of peers wish to join in a debate, the time for it is extended. A peer who opts to speak is certain to have the opportunity to do so: in contrast to the sad experience of many Members, no peer has to go home with an unheard speech in his pocket. A debate tends to become a series of unrelated set-pieces and the element of argument and challenge is missing. Even this mild and peaceful scene can have its lighter moments as when Lord Taylor described an incident on a recent visit to Soviet Russia. 'I was asleep one night and the telephone rang. I picked it up and a voice said, "Good night, good night, good night". I said, "This is Lord Taylor. What do you want?" 'The voice said "are you sleepy darling?" I said "Of course I'm sleepy. You've just woken me" at which she giggled and rang off.'[1]

It is a widely held view that the quality of debate in the Lords

[1] H.L. Deb., Vol. 246, cols. 646–7.

excels over that of the Commons. Yet quality is difficult to define and impossible to measure. The absence of political polemic in the Lords creates a less partial and more constructive atmosphere; calm dignity may seem to give added—and perhaps artificial—value to what is said. However, the Lords who take an active part in debate, mostly the life peers and first-generation peers, have almost all achieved eminence in public life as politicians, diplomats, civil servants or military commanders. Such men may have much to contribute from their store of experience. But their average age is beyond the point of super-annuation. Can they in their declining years really keep pace with the changing complexities of world affairs when they are increasingly removed from the centre of events? Intense engage-ment in the problems of ten and twenty years ago may blinker the outlook on problems of today. Different considerations apply to the clerical members of the Lords. The representatives of the Established Church could supply a moral dimension to the discussion of the international scene. Archbishop Fisher was critical of Government policy at the time of the Suez expedition, and Dr Bell, Bishop of Chichester, actively concerned himself with world problems. But their participation was exceptional; in general, archbishops and bishops are silent or absent when foreign policy is discussed.[1]

While the quality and value of the Lords' debates is a matter for argument, it is certain that their influence has declined. In 1839 Greville remarked to Clarendon, 'As foreign affairs are never discussed except at the House of Lords, you will be much more the public organ of Government than the Foreign Minis-ter himself'.[2] During the nineteenth century the Foreign Secretary was usually in the Lords; today such an appointment is unusual and controversial.[3] Indeed, the Lords have had to struggle to secure any direct representation at the Foreign Office. Earl Stanhope gave up his post as Under-Secretary at the

[1] P. A. Bromhead, *The House of Lords and Contemporary Politics* (Routledge, 1958), pp. 53–67, gives a detailed analysis of the extent to which archbishops and bishops join in the work of the Upper House.

[2] Sir A. W. Ward and G. P. Gooch (eds.) *Cambridge History of British Foreign Policy* (Cambridge U.P., 1922–3), Vol. III, p. 584. Lord Clarendon had just joined the Cabinet as Lord Privy Seal. His speciality was foreign affairs and the Foreign Secretary was in the Commons.

[3] See pp. 69–73 *supra*.

Foreign Office on June 16, 1936, to become the First Commissioner of Works and six weeks later their Lordships complained about the absence of a Foreign Office spokesman.[1] Within a few days the Earl of Plymouth was appointed to succeed Stanhope. Then in 1940 Lord Halifax resigned the Foreign Secretaryship to become Ambassador in Washington and the Lords were left without a Foreign Office representative until 1948, the Government view in foreign affairs debates being presented by various members of their Front Bench.

The Parliament Acts of 1911 and 1949 limited the right of the Lords to determine the content of legislation but, since foreign policy is rarely a matter of legislative form, these Acts are of little significance for the business of the Foreign Office. British Governments have taken less and less notice of votes of opinion in the Lords (as opposed to votes on Bills) since the 1832 Reform Bill. The Government defeat on its Rhodesia policy in December, 1966, was notable mainly for the smallness of the hostile majority, 100 to 84, which demonstrated that the Upper House is not as overwhelmingly Tory as it used to be. An unrepresentative body[2] can scarcely influence the foreign policy of a democratic state. As far as foreign affairs are concerned, the Upper House is little more than an officially supported debating club. Yet their discussions are not without value. The flexibility of their timetable makes it easier for Opposition and backbench peers to obtain a foreign affairs debate. Aspects of the world scene may be ventilated which the Commons have no time to discuss. And the Lords can display quite superbly a spirit of *insouciance*: at the height of the Suez crisis they devoted the greater part of the day to the law of copyright.

[1] H.L. Deb., Vol. 102, cols. 269–76.

[2] The sole representative element in the Lords are the two archbishops and twenty-four bishops of the Established Church. Certainly, the Church is less strong than formerly, but if the clerics intervened forcefully on politically controversial issues, it is arguable that they could seriously embarrass the Government—or the Opposition. The doubts of Archbishop Fisher about Suez and the attitude of Archbishop Ramsey towards the Smith regime in Rhodesia are a pointer to what could happen. There is, however, a strong tradition that the bishops avoid political issues as opposed to moral issues; to put it another way, they avoid moral issues that become a source of party controversy.

CHAPTER VI

Debates 1962-63 – A Case Study

THIS chapter aims to provide a detailed examination of parliamentary debates on foreign affairs in a particular session to illustrate the actual use made of the procedures already described. The choice of session was not easy for no period of parliamentary life is typical. So many factors affect the Westminster scene that it is impossible to define normality.

The session 1962–3 is of special interest because of the obvious variations of opinion within each of the main parties. It would have been an historic period had the Brussels negotiations on Britain's entry into the European Common Market produced a positive conclusion. The veto by General de Gaulle on our membership produced a sense of anti-climax, perhaps tempered by relief in some quarters that great issues had been averted.

The parliamentary year saw great changes in political leadership. After Hugh Gaitskell's death early in 1963, Harold Wilson won a triangular contest with George Brown and Jim Callaghan to become Leader of the Labour Party. Almost at the end of the session the Prime Minister, Harold Macmillan, resigned and was replaced by the Earl of Home who thereupon renounced his peerage. Previously the Earl had been Foreign Secretary, in which office he was succeeded by R. A. Butler. But for virtually the whole of the session under review Foreign Office business in the Commons was the responsibility of the Lord Privy Seal, Edward Heath, who was assisted by J. B. Godber, Minister of State at the Foreign Office, and two Parliamentary Under-Secretaries, Peter Thomas and Peter Smithers. The downfall of Profumo led to the transfer of Godber to become Secretary of State for War and the promotion of Thomas to the rank of Minister of State. To revert to the Opposition, initially Wilson was their 'Shadow' Foreign Secre-

tary but after his elevation to the Leadership this duty passed to
Gordon Walker.

The table below shows that the Commons spent a total of
eighty-six hours forty-two minutes in their Chamber discussing
foreign affairs. This figure is put forward only as a reasonably
accurate approximation since there are insuperable obstacles to
absolute precision. Because this study is concerned essentially
with the business of the Foreign Office, it excludes Commonwealth and Colonial affairs and questions of defence and international trade. But the dividing line between these categories is
wafer-thin and often a matter of opinion. Also while *Hansard*
records the time occupied by each speech in a debate, it does not
show how long is spent on each question, so the figures for
questions are based on an estimate of the time required to fill a
column of *Hansard* in the special conditions of question-time.[1]
The figures below also exclude incidental references to international affairs in debates on other matters, e.g. when the
House should resume sitting after a recess. However, they include the whole of the major Common Market debates although
these covered problems of Commonwealth trade and British
agriculture, because all the speeches were dominated by the
prospect of a major change in the international relationships
of this country.

FOREIGN AFFAIRS ANALYSIS 1962–1963

Date	Procedure	Subject	Time Taken Hrs. Mins.
30 Oct.	Debate on the Address	General discussions including foreign affairs	1·48
31 Oct.	Debate on the Address	Foreign Affairs	7·18
7–8 Nov.	Government Motion	European Economic Community	12·29
9 Nov.	Daily Adjournment Motion	Foreign Service (re Mr MacDermott)	0·30
13 Nov.	Second Reading of Bill	Foreign Compensation Bill	1·55
19 Nov.	Opposition Motion	Nuclear Tests	3·41
22 Nov.	Ministerial Statement	European Communities (Ministerial meetings)	0·35

[1] In order to save time an M.P. asking a question printed on the Order
Paper simply rises in his place and sits down again, but the question appears
in full in *Hansard*.

Parliament and Foreign Affairs

Date	Procedure	Subject	Time Taken Hrs. Mins.
10 Dec.	Approval of a Statutory Instrument	International Coffee Organisation	0·14
11 Dec.	Ministerial Statement	Egypt (Compensation payments)	0·18
12 Dec.	Ten Minute Rule Bill	Foreign Bases (Removal)	0·12
12 Dec.	Report Stage and Third Reading of Bill	Foreign Compensation Bill	0·21
13 Dec.	Adjournment Motion	European Economic Community	2·50
24 Jan.	Ministerial Statement	European Economic Community	0·35
30 Jan.	Ministerial Statement	European Economic Community (Brussels negotiations)	0·33
5 Feb.	Approval of a Statutory Instrument	Egypt (Compensation payments)	2·04
7 Feb.	Second Reading of Consolidated Fund Bill	Congo	3·31
11 Feb.	Ministerial Statement	Iraq	0·07
11–12 Feb.	Government Motion	European Economic Community (Brussels negotiations)	13·48
22 Feb.	Daily Adjournment Motion	Spain (Miss Chloe Vulliamy)	0·29
26 March	Ministerial Statement	N.A.T.O. Council (Foreign Secretary's visit)	0·23
24 April	Ministerial Statement	Laos	0·19
29 April	Ministerial Statement	Fisheries (International Agreements)	0·20
31 May	Whitsun Adjournment Motion	United Nations (Finances)	1·18
21 June	Private Member's Bill Third Reading	Oaths and Evidence (Overseas Authorities and Countries) Bill	0·40
1 July	Ministerial Statement	Harold Philby	0·10
2 July	Ministerial Statement	The Yemen (British Service Personnel)	0·05
2–3 July	Adjournment Motion	Foreign Affairs	12·23
4 July	Ministerial Statement	The Yemen (British Service Personnel)	0·09
15 July	Daily Adjournment Motion	Miss G. M. Lindell	0·23
16 July	Personal Statement by Lord Privy Seal	Missiles in the Middle East	0·02

Debates 1962–63: A Case study

Date	Procedure	Subject	Time Taken Hrs. Mins.
24 July	Third Reading Consolidated Fund (Appropriation) Bill	South Africa (Supply of Arms)	2·16
2 Aug.	Summer Adjournment Motion	U.K. and Eastern Europe (Diplomatic representation)	0·54
		TOTAL	72·40

FOREIGN AFFAIRS ANALYSIS BY PROCEDURE 1962–1963

Procedure	No. of Days on which procedure took place	Time Spent Hrs. Mins.
Debate on the Address	3	9·06
Government Motion	4	26·17
Adjournment Motion	3	15·13
Daily	3	1·22
Summer	1	0·54
Whitsun	1	1·18
Opposition Motion	1	3·41
Government Bill	2	2·16
Consolidated Fund Bill	2	5·47
Private Member's Bills	2	0·52
Approval of a Statutory Instrument	2	2·18
Ministerial Statement	11	3·34
Personal Statement	1	0·02
Questions	see below	14·02
TOTAL		86·42

TIME SPENT ON QUESTIONS

Type of Question	Occasions	No. of answers	Time Spent Hrs. Mins.
Foreign Office	18	184	8·25
Prime Minister	50	97	4·43
Private notice	6	6	0·32
Answered at end of questions	2	8	0·22
Written answers	—	439	—
TOTALS		734	14·02

103

The total time of nearly eighty-seven hours represents, again roughly, about two and a half weeks of the time of the Commons. During the 1962–3 session the House sat for thirty-three weeks so, irrespective of all the approximations that must be made, it is evident that Members spent but a small proportion of their time on foreign affairs. That this is not untypical is shown by parallel statistical analysis of other sessions that appear in the Appendix.[1] Indeed, the calculation above tends to over-estimate the amount of attention Members devote to foreign policy since it ignores committee work outside the Chamber. A great deal of time is occupied by official committees, especially in connection with financial matters and the detail of proposed legislation: there is almost no such committee work associated with international affairs.

There were four major foreign policy debates in this session. As usual one day of the debate on the Address was devoted to international affairs. On this occasion Members concentrated on two themes, the Cuba crisis, which had just been successfully surmounted, and the Chinese invasion of India. The most noteworthy speech came from Harold Wilson, then 'Shadow' Foreign Minister, who suggested that Britain might send arms to India on a 'lease-lend' basis reminiscent of the Second World War. The other general foreign policy discussion did not come until the beginning of July, 1963, when Members spent two days largely on argument about nuclear weapons in relation to NATO and their effect on relations with Western Germany and the Soviet Union. Two more two-day debates arose from the Common Market negotiations. The first, in November, 1962, related to the terms which the Government might accept to join the Treaty of Rome, and gave Edward Heath, the Minister in direct charge of the negotiations, a peculiarly awkward task. His speech had to satisfy two potentially conflicting desiderata. To British opinion he had to stress the Government's strength of purpose in pursuing its European policy. To observers on the continent he had to show determination to obtain acceptable terms for entry, especially in relation to New Zealand produce and the continuation of agricultural deficiency payments in this country. The second discussion, in February, 1963, was arranged

[1] pp. 177–8 *infra*.

104

to examine the new situation caused by the collapse of the nego-tiations; the second day for this debate was provided by the Opposition sacrificing a Consolidated Fund Bill day. Both these Common Market debates ended with divisions that gave the Government a majority of approximately one hundred, a fair reflection of party strengths in the Commons at that time. In November, 1962, the Liberals, strongly in favour of joining the Common Market, voted with the Government, but in February, 1963, they abstained. There was no division at the July debate. A vote always takes place at the end of the debate on the Address, but in 1962 it was related to an Opposition amend-ment on unemployment and had no connection with the earlier discussion on foreign affairs.

Close study of *Hansard* often reveals substantial differences of opinion within each of the major parties. The Common Market issue produced a complex pattern of attitudes which had little relation to the orthodox Conservative-Labour polarity. Some Labour Members were keen 'Europeans'; some Conserva-tives were 'Commonwealth men'. Other Conservatives were agitated about how British agriculture would be affected by union with Europe. Divergences of view existed on the opposi-tion front-bench, and in the November debate it was clear that Hugh Gaitskell was more critical of Government policy than George Brown. Parallel variations on the Government front-bench—if they existed—were naturally not allowed to appear in public debate. But these doubts about the wisdom of party policy did not affect Members when the time came to vote and party discipline was observed at the end of both Common Market debates, except that one or two unorthodox Conserva-tives were absent when the division was called in November. A month later no fewer than 47 Conservative backbenchers, including a number of ex-Ministers, placed a motion on the Order Paper critical of ministerial keenness to join the Common Market. Clearly, party loyalty was under great strain. Since the Brussels negotiations collapsed, the climax was avoided, and it is a matter for speculation whether the issue could have pro-voked a serious split in the Conservative Party. So long as no finality was reached the dissidents could always claim that, by stressing the need to safeguard British and Commonwealth interests, they were strengthening Heath's position at the negotiating table by showing that unfavourable terms would be unacceptable to British opinion.

In the debate that followed the collapse of the talks in Brussels, ministerial speeches were curiously forlorn. Their chosen avenue had been blocked and there had been no time to discover alternatives. Macmillan announced that Princess Margaret's visit to Paris had been cancelled on his advice for political reasons and admitted that the official reason for the cancellation, the need to keep a sufficient number of Councillors of State in the country, had been a diplomatic white lie. Wilson described all this as petty and peevish. Yet the political tension had disappeared since Members could slip comfortably back into normal party associations. A Conservative backbencher, H. Price (Lewisham, West), who asked whether Ministers could provide the leadership that the country required, still voted for the Government.

Speeches of Members in the Chamber make frequent reference to their travels abroad. In the July debate Sir Cyril Osborne (Con. Louth) reported on his visit to Russia as Chairman of the Anglo-Soviet Parliamentary Group which had sent a delegation to Moscow during the Whitsun recess. He stressed the Russian desire for friendship with Britain and their fear of German re-armament, especially in relation to nuclear weapons. Sir Cyril is commonly thought of as a right-wing Tory, but almost the whole of this speech could well have come from the Labour benches. The fact that a Member had led a parliamentary delegation abroad may well help him to catch the Speaker's eye. Privy Councillors also have some priority, and they provided thirteen out of the seventy-nine backbench speeches in the four debates under review.[1] Otherwise the contributions were as varied as possible, and a Member with unorthodox or extreme views seems to have an above-average chance of being heard. The table below shows that roughly equal numbers of speeches come from the Government and Opposition benches, and that Labour speeches tend to be rather longer. It is also the case that the lengthiest backbench contributions of all came from Labour left-wingers: K. Zilliacus (Manchester, Gorton) occupied

[1] The proportion of Privy Councillors, who are usually ex-Ministers, on the backbenches is quite small. During this session there were 28 Privy Councillors among approximately 500 backbenchers.

NUMBER AND LENGTH OF SPEECHES

Type of Speech	31 Oct. 1962		7–8 Nov. 1962		11–12 Feb. 1963		2–3 July 1963	
	No. of speakers	Average in minutes	No. of speakers	Average in minutes	No. of speakers	Average in minutes	No. of speakers	Average in minutes
Ministerial	2	36½	3[1]	45	4	43	4	37½
Opposition front-bench	2	36	4	42	4	41½	4	33
Government backbench	7	19	12	17½	11	17	10	19
Opposition backbench	6	25	9	22	11	20	9	27
Liberal	1	21	1	30	1	23	1	30

[1] On this occasion the Government did not provide a front-bench spokesman to wind up the first day's debate. Instead there was a longer-than-average contribution (36 minutes) from a Conservative backbencher, Sir Alexander Spearman (Scarborough and Whitby).

forty-four minutes in the July debate and J. Mendelson (Penistone) required forty minutes.

Apart from the major debates analysed above, there were five other opportunities each lasting more than an hour to discuss international questions. In November an Opposition motion objected to the Government proposal to resume nuclear tests; the Commons spent half a day on this topic and rejected the motion by 299 votes to 224, the Liberals joining the Labour Opposition. In December the adjournment motion device was used for another half-day examination of the progress of the Brussels negotiations. Various doubts were expressed by Sir Anthony Hurd (Con. Newbury). This speech was highly significant as Sir Anthony was recognised to be an influential spokesman for agricultural interests. It was public evidence of the weight of agricultural pressure being exerted on Ministers— the part of the iceberg above the level of the sea. In February Right-wing Conservatives led by J. Biggs-Davison (Chigwell) used the second reading of the Consolidated Fund Bill to object to Government support for United Nations' actions in the Congo. Again, this was visible evidence of much private pressure, the iceberg in this case being the so-called 'Katanga Lobby'. Division of opinion on the Congo had no relation to party, and the Opposition supported the Government. The Whitsun adjournment allowed J. Woollam (Con. Liverpool, West Derby) to raise the financial problems of the United Nations and produced a broad measure of agreement on the need to support the organisation. Finally, in July the Third Reading of the Consolidated Fund Bill demonstrated Labour and Liberal concern about the supply of arms to South Africa and one of the two Conservative backbench speakers (Humphry Berkeley, Lancaster) was also critical of Government policy. To summarise these debates, one was a party dog-fight, one was largely uncontroversial, while in the other three the pattern of opinions did not match the party affiliations of Members.

Traditionally the House of Commons is prepared to give attention to the grievances of individuals. Usually such complaints will concern Departments dealing with domestic matters, but in the 1962–3 session three personal cases came within the responsibility of the Foreign Office. Anthony Greenwood (Lab. Rossendale) enquired into the circumstances that led to the compulsory retirement of an official in the Foreign Service. Sir Leslie Plummer (Lab. Deptford) described the treatment that a British tourist had received from the Spanish police. Airey Neave (Con. Abingdon) complained about the long delay in obtaining compensation for a British victim of Nazi persecution. There can be no doubt that this form of parliamentary activity has an effect on the care with which the Foreign Office—and other Departments—deal with personal cases.

Members produce a large and steady flow of questions on foreign affairs. It is difficult to state an exact number since the boundary between foreign affairs and other subjects, notably defence, is difficult to define. All questions dealt with by Foreign Office Ministers must obviously be included in the total, but in the case of the Prime Minister's questions the categories become indistinct. There are also questions ostensibly about foreign affairs which are asked in order that supplementaries may be put to make party debating points.[1] My estimate is that during the 1962–3 session 443 questions dealing with foreign affairs obtained oral answers in the Commons. A further 439 queries received a written answer in *Hansard*, most of which had failed to get a reply in the Chamber owing to shortage of time. The number of oral answers, 295, is lower than the total of questions since two or more similar questions may receive a joint reply.

Leading members of the Opposition frontbench rarely ask questions but they sometimes join in the supplementary exchanges following the more important answers. The same is true of the Liberal leader, Jo Grimond. All significant international events of the period were raised, although the balance of interest between the parties differed considerably. The favourite Con-

[1] For example H.C. Deb., Vol. 679, col. 642. 'Mr Lipton (Lab. Brixton) asked the Prime Minister whether, in view of the widespread opinion that the time is not opportune, he will ask President Kennedy to defer his visit to this country for the time being.

The Prime Minister: No, Sir.

Mr Lipton: If the visit is still on, does not the Prime Minister think that the President should be given the opportunity of exchanging views with a new Prime Minister and not a Prime Minister who is under notice to quit and whose political status at home and abroad is inevitably impaired. The Prime Minister: The hon. Gentleman has made his point in a way that is characteristic of him, and with his usual courtesy, and I leave it at that'.

servative topic was the activities of the United Nations in the Congo. Labour backbenchers were concerned about various aspects of United States policy and about nuclear tests. Naturally the largest share of questions came from the Opposition.

FOREIGN AFFAIRS ORAL QUESTIONS: PARTY ORIGIN

Party	No. of questions	No. of questioners
Labour	348	66
Conservative	88	35
Liberal	6	4
Independent	1	1
TOTALS	443	106

Biggs-Davison was the most active Conservative in this field with 15 questions, but his party colleagues were almost all content with one, two or three. The following list shows the Labour Members who scored more than ten oral answers:

A. Henderson	35	S. Swingler	13
K. Zilliacus	26	C. Mayhew	12
J. Rankin	22	P. Noel-Baker	12
W. Warbey	22	E. Shinwell	12
F. Allaun	18	Mrs B. Castle	10
T. Driberg	14	E. Hughes	10
J. Stonehouse	13		

It will be noted that frequent intervention at question-time is not a passport to ministerial office. None of the top six listed above found a place in the Wilson administration of 1964: apart from Henderson they are noted for their left-wing sympathies. No doubt the nature of their opinions led both to their vigour with questions and their subsequent exclusion from the Labour Government. The figures also show something of how Members specialize in their interests and how they make very unequal claims on the time and attention of the House.[1] The thirteen Labour Members named above together with Biggs-Davison were responsible for just over half the total of oral questions on foreign affairs.

[1] On this point see also my *Honourable Members*, 2nd ed. (Faber, 1964), p. 81.

No fewer than eleven ministerial statements were made to the Commons relating to foreign affairs. Three were concerned with the Common Market negotiations and two with the detention of British servicemen in the Yemen following a frontier violation. The other six subjects were—Egypt compensation payments, recognition of the new Iraq government, the projected NATO multilateral nuclear force, negotiations with the Soviet Union as co-chairmen of the Geneva Laos conference to end fighting in that country, withdrawal from two nineteenth-century conventions over fishing limits and the admission that Philby was the 'third man' in the Foreign Office who had warned Burgess and Maclean in 1951. The last of these items was essentially a Foreign Office staffing matter. All but one of these statements were made by Edward Heath. (The exception which dealt with the Yemen, came from Peter Thomas, Minister of State at the Foreign Office). They were followed by a few minutes of questions which came mainly from the Opposition front bench and from the Liberal leader Jo Grimond. Opposition leaders may have some foreknowledge of what a Minister is to say and so have an opportunity to prepare their interrogation. Ministerial replies are cautious and reluctant to go far beyond the terms of the initial pronouncement. Especially will a Minister be careful not to stray into the area of responsibility of another Department; Thomas refused to make any comment upon the military aspect of the Yemen incident.[1] Usually the Minister making the statement is left to deal with the subsequent questioning, but after Heath had announced the final breakdown of the Common Market negotiations, Prime Minister Macmillan joined in the following exchanges to agree that a full-scale debate should be held.

These eleven statements varied greatly in importance. The end of the Common Market negotiations was a truly historic moment: the incursion of a handful of British troops into Yemeni territory faded rapidly from the public memory. So the problem arises how an event is judged to merit a parliamentary statement. What are the criteria? It would seem that there are no firm rules to be applied. Basically this is a political decision to be influenced by the contemporary political climate and the

[1] H.C. Deb., Vol. 680, cols. 602–3.

Parliament and Foreign Affairs

extent to which Ministers feel it to be proper or desirable to keep the public fully informed. As the significance of events changes with the passage of time, it is difficult to assess these matters in retrospect. By now the Yemeni frontier incident does not appear worthy of two ministerial statements. Yet in July, 1963, it caused much concern, partly on account of the well-being of the men involved, partly because it seemed to show incompetence by the British military authorities in Aden and partly was it due to the irritation of Left-wing opinion by the Macmillan Government's refusal to accord recognition to the republican regime in the Yemen.

1962–3 was a little unusual in that it provides no examples of Bills designed to implement international agreements; this has but a small effect on the time analysis set out above since such Bills are often uncontroversial and pass easily through the Chamber. Had the Common Market negotiations produced agreement, the whole parliamentary timetable for the remainder of the session would have suffered a revolution. As it was the Foreign Office produced only one measure, the Foreign Compensation Bill, which was essentially of domestic concern. It authorized the Foreign Compensation Commission to distribute money received from the British Government to claimants who suffered loss during the Suez incident: previously the Commission's work had been confined to the distribution of monies received from foreign governments. The Bill also authorized the payment of pensions to the staff of the Commission. It was uncontroversial and there was no division on the Second Reading. One other Bill became law that fell within the ambit of the Foreign Office, the Oaths and Evidence (Overseas Authorities and Countries) Bill, which was introduced by a backbencher, Biggs-Davison. This was so technical and uncontroversial that it went through the Second Reading 'on the nod', i.e. there was no discussion at all. A brief debate took place on the Third Reading which did little more than recognise the existence of the measure before it was passed. Another private member's Bill introduced under the ten minute rule by Emrys Hughes (Lab. South Ayrshire) was designed to remove the United States' Polaris submarine base in Scotland. After a short speech in its favour and a short speech against, the Bill was rejected by 177 votes to 34; Government supporters opposed the Bill, the Left-wing of the Labour Party voted for it while the majority of Labour Members abstained.

Two Statutory Instruments were discussed during the session, both under the confirmatory resolution procedure. The International Coffee Organisation Order excited little interest; its purpose was to exempt from income tax the staff of this new Organisation which was about to be established in London. Employees of international organisations commonly enjoy tax reliefs from the host country and these arrangements are reciprocal. The other Order was issued under the Foreign Compensation Act noticed above and represented the culmination of years of controversy within the Conservative Party over the payment of compensation for assets nationalized and sequestrated by Egypt at the time of the Suez operation. Under an Agreement reached in 1959 the Egyptian Government agreed to pay £27,500,000 in compensation for the loss of these British assets. The total of claims for recompense was considerably in excess of this figure and, after years of prodding and pushing from the interests concerned, the British Government agreed to provide additional money to add to the compensation fund. As a result the Foreign Compensation Commission was enabled to meet in full agreed claims up to £10,000 but the larger claimants were able to recoup progressively smaller proportions of their losses. The terms of this settlement were denounced as inadequate by a number of Conservative Members, some of whom admitted in their speeches that they had a financial interest in the companies adversely affected. Although the Order was the immediate responsibility of the Foreign Office and although the root of the problem was—at least in part—the action of a foreign government, the issue was not one of foreign policy. Rather was it how far the British Government should force the British taxpayer to make good losses to individuals and firms incurred through its Suez policy.

Comment on the influence of Commons' debates will be postponed until the final chapter. But it must be noted here that limited discussions on a particular topic are frequently more impressive than the day-long reviews of the whole international scene. General foreign affairs debates tend to be disappointing. Their subject-matter is so broad that attention given to problems is uneven. One speech may have little relation to that which preceded it, and a series of disconnected contributions scarcely constitutes 'debate' in the ordinary sense of that word. And since backbench speeches are limited in number and diverse in both content and attitude, it is rarely possible to sense dominant trends of opinion from what is said. An examination of a precise topic, e.g. Egyptian compensation or the United Nations' activities in the Congo is potentially more rewarding. A higher level of information is introduced, the speeches have a common theme with constant inter-relation; they may also be briefer and consequently more incisive. The total effect can be to present the Minister winding up the debate with a formidable case to answer, whereas discursive talk helps to blunt the severity of criticism of Ministers in the major debates.

The table of foreign policy discussions in the House of Lords has many similarities to the parallel list for the Commons on pp. 101–3. Major developments in the international scene were considered more or less simultaneously in the two Houses. But the Lords had no two-day debates and they also found time to talk about some topics that did not attract much attention in the Commons, e.g. the problems of refugees in relation to the World Refugee Year and the operation of our overseas information services. These subjects could be fitted in to the Lords' time-table because its greater flexibility provides opportunities to discuss non-ministerial motions: there were eight such motions during the session, two were introduced by Lord Henderson, the Labour front-bench spokesman on foreign affairs, and the remaining six originated from backbenchers.

FOREIGN AFFAIRS ANALYSIS: HOUSE OF LORDS 1962–1963

Date	Procedure	Subject	Time Spent Hrs. Mins.
1 Nov.	Address in reply to Her Majesty's Speech	Foreign Policy	4·35
8 Nov.	Government Motion	Britain and the Common Market	6·56
13 Nov.	Ministerial Statement	Retirement of Mr McDermott	0·12
15 Nov.	Motion (Viscount Astor)	The Refugee Problem	3·14

Debates 1962–63: A Case study

Date	Procedure	Subject	Time Spent Hrs. Mins.
3 Dec.	Approval of a Statutory Instrument	International Coffee Organisation Order, 1962	0·09
11 Dec.	Ministerial Statement	British Subjects' Egyptian Claims	0·12
18 Dec.	Second Reading of Bill	Foreign Compensation Bill	1·47
24 Jan.	Ministerial Statement	Common Market Negotiations	0·18
6 Feb.	Motion (Lord Henderson)	The International Situation	5·27
7 Feb.	Approval of a Statutory Instrument	Foreign Compensation (Egypt) (Final Distribution) Order	1·14
11 Feb.	Ministerial Statement	Britain and Iraq	0·03
13 Feb.	Motion (Lord Crathorne)	N.A.T.O. and European Unity	3·50
20 Feb.	Motion (Lord Ogmore)	A United Nations Force	3·34
6 March	Motion (Lord Williams of Barnburgh)	Consequences of Breakdown of Brussels Negotiations	5·44
21 March	Motion (Lord Kennet)	Visas for East German Scientists and Artistes	1·24
26 March	Ministerial Statement	Foreign Secretary's Visit to N.A.T.O.	0·13
26 March	Motion (Viscount Massereene & Ferrard)	The Overseas Information Services	3·55
29 April	Ministerial Statement	Fishery Limits and Trade in Fish	0·17
30 May	Ministerial Statement	Laos	0·06
24 June	Ministerial Statement	Incident in the Yemen	0·07
26 June	Motion (Lord Henderson	The International Situation	6·43
28 June	Second Reading of Bill	Oaths and Evidence (Overseas Authorities and Countries) Bill	0·05
1 July	Ministerial Statement	The Disappearance of Mr Philby	0·08
2 July	Ministerial Statement	British Prisoners in the Yemen	0·02
4 July	Ministerial Statement	The Yemen: Release of British Prisoners	0·06
26 July	Ministerial Statement	Nuclear Test Ban Treaty	0·06
		TOTAL	50·27

FOREIGN AFFAIRS ANALYSIS—BY PROCEDURE
HOUSE OF LORDS, 1962–1963

Type of procedure	No. of Days on which procedure took place	Time Spent Hrs. Mins.
Address in reply to Her Majesty's Speech	1	4·35
Government Motion	1	6·56
Motion	8	33·51
Approval of a Statutory Instrument	2	1·23
Government Bills	2	1·52
Ministerial Statements	12	1·50
Questions	see below	3·28
TOTALS		53·55

FOREIGN AFFAIRS, ANALYSIS OF QUESTIONS
HOUSE OF LORDS, 1962–1963

Type of Question	No. of Days	No. of Questions	Time Spent Hrs. Mins.
Ordinary Oral Answer Question	29	33	2·58
Private Notice Question	5	5	0·30
Written Answers	—	8	—
TOTALS		46	3·28

The number of questions in the Lords is infinitesimal compared with the flood in the Commons. Since they are treated
more leisurely and are not designed for party purposes, a
Lords question may well produce more information than one in
the Commons. Total time devoted to foreign affairs in the Lords
was 62% of that in the Commons. However, any comparison
must remember that the Lords sit for far less time; they met on
four days a week instead of five, all-night sittings are unknown
and, indeed, on the average day debates continue for about half
as long as in the Commons. Thus their Lordships actually spent
a greater proportion of their time on foreign affairs, no doubt
because they give less detailed attention to other matters,
especially finance. It has been shown above that controversy in
the Commons on foreign policy was muted and sometimes
crossed party lines. The harmony in the Lords was even more
noticeable. Only one vote on a foreign policy issue was recorded:
the Government won a division at the end of the Common
Market debate by sixty-two votes to twenty-three.

CHAPTER VII

Political Pressures

THE House of Commons is surrounded by a network of political pressures; some are hidden, some are open but not widely known, some are highly publicised. It is convenient to think of this network as a pyramid. At the top are the Prime Minister and his Cabinet colleagues who are finally responsible for making decisions on national policy. At the base are the local branches of organizations that wish to influence the decisions made at the top, and in between are the national bodies of these organizations. The most influential associations, e.g. the major political parties, must be thought of as occupying a higher place in the pyramid nearer to the nation's leadership. In this structure political pressures are thrust up from below all the time. Often those near the base of the pyramid will communicate directly with those at the apex, but this may be done as a publicity-seeking gesture rather than out of real hope of exerting influence. Usually it is better tactics for the uninfluential to attempt to win the sympathy of those half-way up the pyramid, e.g. Members of Parliament. Alternatively, they may seek to win over an important organization to their viewpoint, e.g. the CND campaign to capture the Labour Party in 1960.

Thus a Member is a gatekeeper for political pressures. He receives representations from his constituency, and from various organizations: some of these will be passed upward to Ministers. Inevitably, a Member will pay greatest heed to those organizations which give him greatest support, notably the association of his constituency party or perhaps a trade union. He will also pay special attention to communications with which he has general sympathy for political, financial or religious reasons. This pattern of activity has been fully described in the literature of

117

pressure group studies,[1] which has been largely devoted to domestic issues. However, the present task is to examine its operation in the context of foreign affairs. Finally, it must be noted that pressures also work downwards in the pyramid. Party leaders urge their followers to accept policy decisions already reached. In Parliament it is the task of the Whips to retain the loyalty of backbenchers.

CONSTITUENCY AND PARTY OPINION

Every Member of the Commons owes a great debt to his local party organisation. His political life depends entirely on constituency support. His selection as a candidate, the cost of his election campaign, canvassing and the other chores of electioneering, all these depend on the will and the sacrifice of party activists. No individual can hope to win a seat without the assistance of a substantial political organisation. Clearly in this situation a Member is vulnerable to pressure; his political career will almost certainly be ruined should his constituency association become so displeased that it decides to choose another candidate. Such a threat rarely develops because the behaviour of local political associations is conditioned by restraint and apathy and so not often do they find cause to complain of their Members.

Constituency dissatisfaction with a Member can never be measured. Should a Member neglect local affairs or take some controversial action—how many people know, and how many care? Between elections no referendum is ever held on a national issue: the 'recall' is unknown to the British Constitution.[2] But a Member's position can be seriously challenged by a relatively small number of his nominal supporters. Effective influence can be exerted by those who hold positions of authority in his local association. A constituency Labour Party is controlled by a General Management Committee composed of representatives

---

[1] See e.g. S. E. Finer, *Anonymous Empire* (Pall Mall, 1958); M. Harrison, *Trade Unions and the Labour Party* (Allen & Unwin, 1960); A. Potter, *Organised Groups in British National Politics* (Faber, 1961); J. D. Stewart, *British Pressure Groups* (O.U.P., 1958).

[2] The 'recall' is a device used in a few States in the U.S.A. whereby a petition signed by a given proportion of voters has the effect of making an elective office vacant. The incumbent can defend his stewardship by contesting the ensuing by-election.

of ward and parish organizations and of representatives of affiliated organizations, mainly local trade union branches. The business of the GMC is directed by an executive committee. Similarly in the Conservative Party authority at the constituency level is concentrated in a local executive committee, but a Conservative Association does hold infrequent general meetings open to all its members which are normally occasions for berating political opponents rather than the ventilation of intra-party disharmony. Thus it is not the public at large which puts pressure on Members; nor is it usually the mass membership of a political association. Rather is it a few opinion-leaders among local supporters who tend to express displeasure in private conversation or correspondence. Since pressure can be exerted quietly, especially by Conservatives, the volume of such activity cannot be known. However, if the tension is caused by a policy issue that arouses deep feeling, some public outburst is inevitable.

The amount of conflict between Members and their local supporters should not be exaggerated.[1] Especially on foreign affairs a Member will have more information than the executive committee of his constituency party and, since events abroad do not generally arouse widespread feeling, his views on international issues tend to go unchallenged. Almost every Member commands a degree of genuine respect and policy issues cause conflict only if he deviates from the party line or—conceivably— if local opinion is opposed to orthodox or national party opinion.

A Conservative Member in conflict with his local executive may appeal to his local association; not infrequently such an appeal is successful. In 1952 the Executive of the South Dorset Conservative Association passed a resolution of no confidence in their Member, Viscount Hinchingbrooke, because he opposed the policy of the Churchill Government on the re-arming of Western Germany. A meeting of the Association supported Hinchingbrooke and the Executive resigned. This case is unusual in that it does not fit into the normal Left-Right polarity. The usual form of tussle is a contest between Right and Left wing opinion within the party. The dedicated party supporters

[1] For a detailed account see Austin Ranney, *Pathways to Parliament* (Macmillan, 1965).

who form the core of constituency parties tend to be extreme in their attitudes, i.e. Right-wing Conservative or Left-wing Labour. Members who get into trouble, therefore, tend to be those with moderate opinions and appear to their critics to have some sympathy with the opposing party.

The Suez Crisis of 1956 led to two rebellions in the Conservative Party. One small group of Members refused to support military action against Egypt and abstained from voting in a division: another larger group of fifteen abstained in a division after the decision to withdraw from Port Said was announced, and eight of these Members resigned the Conservative whip in May, 1957, when British ships started again to use the Canal. It is instructive to compare the treatment meted out to the two rebel bands by their constituency parties.[1] Nigel Nicolson, the most outspoken of those who opposed the Suez invasion, was rejected by the Bournemouth East and Christchurch Conservative Association which decided by a majority of three to one to seek another candidate for the next election. Other Conservative Members who shared Nicolson's view received varying treatment. Relations between Sir Frank Medlicott (Central Norfolk) and his local Association were badly strained and Sir Frank announced that he would not contest the next election. At Birmingham (Handsworth) Sir Edward Boyle[2] fared rather better: a statement issued by the Handsworth Conservative Association recognized the right of a Conservative Member to act in accordance with his sincere convictions. Three other Conservatives were treated with reasonable tolerance, but in each case there were special circumstances to help them. J. J. Astor (Plymouth, Sutton) had already announced that he did not intend to contest the next election. Sir Robert Boothby (East Aberdeenshire) had represented the constituency since 1924 and as a politician of national reputation he had an immensely strong personal position. William Yates (The Wrekin) had a

[1] Cf. Leon D. Epstein, *British Politics in the Suez Crisis* (University of Illinois Press, 1964) and Nigel Nicolson's very fair account of his own experience, *People and Parliament* (Weidenfeld and Nicolson, 1958).

[2] In November, 1956, Sir Edward resigned his post as Economic Secretary to the Treasury on the Suez issue: in January, 1957, he was appointed Parliamentary Secretary to the Ministry of Education in the Macmillan Government but he did not recant from his earlier views.

majority of a mere 478 votes, so any serious dispute in the local party seemed likely to present the seat to the Opposition. Anthony Nutting (Con. Melton), who resigned as Minister of State for Foreign Affairs over the Suez issue, also gave up his seat in the Commons: the Melton association sent a message of support to the Prime Minister without giving Nutting an opportunity to defend his opinions. Nutting was, therefore, condemned unheard.

The fate of the Right-wing rebels, those who objected to normalization after the fiasco of the invasion, can be described more briefly. Although their offence was greater, since resignation of the whip is a graver step than abstention in a single division, none of them was in serious trouble. Angus Maude suffered the biggest challenge and he obtained a vote of confidence from his Association at South Ealing by 572 votes to 28.[1]

An exactly parallel situation developed over the issue of oil sanctions against Rhodesia. In a Commons' division on December 22, 1965, Conservatives split into three sections. The front-bench advice was to abstain, but fifty Members voted against the imposition of oil sanctions while thirty-one others voted in support of the Labour Government's policy of applying sanctions. No constituency reaction was reported against the fifty Right-wing Tories, but some of the thirty-one had subsequently to face local hostility, notably the leader of this group Richard Hornby (Tonbridge) who was formerly a Parliamentary Under-Secretary at the Commonwealth Relations Office, Angus Maude (Stratford-on-Avon) and Terence Higgins (Worthing). Maude's case was complicated by articles he wrote for *Encounter* and the *Spectator* which contained general criticism of the emphasis in Conservative policy and which led to his resignation from the 'Shadow Government'; however, it is probable that Stratford Conservatives were at least as irritated by his vote on Rhodesian oil as they were by his articles. The Worthing case was even more complex. A Member challenged by local supporters on a particular issue has a stock response—that there is no evidence of the view of his constituency party as a whole. Local Conservative Associations do not often pass resolutions on a specific topic which are con-

[1] Ranney, *op cit.*, p. 85.

troversial among Conservatives. But some Worthing Conservatives had strong feelings over Rhodesia, and before the crucial vote in the Commons the Worthing Association had held a general meeting which condemned all sanctions against the Smith regime. Thus Higgins' vote was cast in defiance of the known view of his local Association, and his Association was itself in conflict with official Conservative policy. The outcome was about forty resignations from the Worthing Conservative Association and the appearance of a Right-wing Independent Conservative candidate at the 1966 Election. Higgins was re-elected without difficulty, his Right-wing opponent obtained 1,044 votes and lost his deposit.

There are few conflicts to record between Labour Members and their constituencies on foreign policy. Labour Members who rebel against party policy are usually Left-wing and since their local party executives tend to be Left-wing also few conflicts arise. No doubt, any vote against the Wilson Government in the 1964–6 Parliament would have caused trouble because of the small parliamentary majority. But the tension that faces Left-wing Labour Members is not with their constituency parties, but with the Whips, the Party leadership and Transport House. The Left-wingers who lost the Whip in 1954 for voting against the London and Paris agreements were in no danger from their local associations, and in 1949 the Gateshead Labour Party still defended Konni Zilliacus when he was no longer acceptable to Transport House. Conversely, a Right-wing rebel who seems to share some Conservative attitudes will soon face local hostility: Stanley Evans (Wednesbury) who supported the Suez invasion was called on to resign by his constituency party—and did so.

Pressure from local opinion leaders has the greatest effect when a party is deeply divided on an issue that arouses deep feeling. There are divergencies of view within both main parties on the question of joining the Common Market, but this controversy has never set a constituency aflame since it fails to kindle widespread passion. Rhodesia is a complete contrast. The problem is, or appears to be, much simpler. For some it is a moral issue, for others, usually Conservatives, their families or business interests are involved. The pressure against the Hornby-Higgins group was highly significant as a reflection of Tory opinion: it should not be under-estimated merely because the pressure eased in face of a General Election and the need to maintain a facade of party unity. Indeed, the Rhodesian oil sanctions dispute raises the question of how far constituency attitudes may affect a Member's action when his party is in disarray. Approximately one-sixth of Conservative Members voted against oil sanctions, but this statement conceals regional variations. In Devon and Cornwall there is a strong body of liberal opinion: only one of the dozen Conservative representatives from this area voted against the oil sanctions—Greville Howard (St Ives) who had already decided to retire at the next election. In Hampshire there is a considerable concentration of Service personnel, retired colonial officials and wealthy persons likely to have financial interests abroad: half of the Conservative Members from this area voted against oil sanctions. (The strongest reactions against the pro-sanctions Conservatives came from constituencies with a similar social composition.) These proportions suggest that when party unity is broken there can be a relationship between how a Member votes and the type of constituency he represents. Such a correlation could be explained in one of two ways. A Conservative Association excessively Right-wing in outlook might take great care to choose a Right-wing candidate. With an occasional exception, this does not happen because selection committees tend to pick whoever seems to them the best candidate judged in terms of personal qualities and experience rather than in terms of opinion. The more probable explanation stems from how a Member reacts when confronted with the unusual situation that his vote is not predetermined by party loyalty. If he has strong personal feelings, he will vote as his conscience dictates; if not, he may well be influenced by recent conversations with his leading local supporters.

The attitude of Members towards constituency pressure on matters of policy is ambiguous. On the one hand they commonly invoke the spirit of Burke: on the other hand they accept that local parties, especially those that are large and active, must be treated with tact. One of the more cynical maxims of parliamentary life is that a Member who does not keep his constituency happy is a fool.

Any assessment of the impact of constituency opinion on party policy must consider the possibility of it having a direct effect at national level, so by-passing Members of Parliament. The Labour Party has a tradition that principles of policy are determined in democratic fashion at its National Conference composed of representatives of constituency parties and affiliated organizations. This concept was badly dented at Scarborough in 1960 when Hugh Gaitskell as Party Leader refused to accept the Conference resolution in favour of nuclear disarmament. Sustained by a majority of the Parliamentary Labour Party, Gaitskell remained Leader and he secured a reversal of the nuclear disarmament decision at the 1961 Conference. Up to 1960 there had been no major clash between the Party Leader and the Annual Conference, but in 1932 George Lansbury ignored a joint resolution of the National Executive of the Party acting with the TUC which favoured an economic boycott of Japan owing to her actions in Manchuria.[1] Laski's activities as Chairman of the National Executive caused great irritation to Prime Minister Attlee. In 1946 Laski was reported to have stated in a foreign journal that 'the Labour Government would if necessary bring economic pressure to bear on Spain'. In a private letter to Laski, Attlee commented 'You have no right whatever to speak on behalf of the Government . . . a period of silence on your part would be welcome'.[2] At the Labour Party Conference of 1966 two resolutions on foreign affairs were passed contrary to the wishes of the executive; one of these called for reductions in military expenditure east of Suez and the other urged the Labour Cabinet to bring pressure on the United States to stop the Vietnam war. Prime Minister Wilson commented on these motions, 'While we are always keen to know the views of Conference, the Government is, of course, responsible to Parliament. It would not be possible to run a coherent foreign policy or defence policy if you could be forced to change direction, perhaps even to break treaties and alliances, on the basis of a single vote.' These examples show that Labour Leaders, in or out of office, pay little attention to views on foreign policy expressed through the Party organization. The National Executive must approve the Party's election manifestoes, but in 1966 this appeared to be nothing more than

[1] R. Bassett, *Democracy and Foreign Policy* (London School of Economics, 1952), p. 552.
[2] K. Martin, *Harold Laski* (Gollancz, 1953), p. 182.

a hasty rubber-stamping of a draft prepared under the supervision of the Prime Minister.

It is tempting, therefore, to write off the idea of intra-party democracy in the Labour Party as a sham.[1] Yet the temptation should be at least partially resisted. The idea that their Party is democratic—more democratic than the Tories—has a firm hold on active Labour supporters. Labour has a strong tradition of discussing differences openly and of coming to decisions by vote. The resolutions in 1960 and 1966 against the Leadership were passed by relatively small majorities. In 1966 the Amalgamated Engineering Union changed sides on the critical resolutions and this carried the day; the AEU decision was unexpected and was probably due to the absence of its President, Sir William Carron. A Conference vote that depends on the absence of one man is unlikely to make a Government change its policy: were a hostile majority substantial, it could be more influential. Conference resolutions also must have an effect on the Parliamentary Labour Party. It becomes impossible to threaten to withdraw the whip from a critical Left-wing Member for merely advocating policies that have secured the assent of the Party Conference. If a fundamental clash between the Labour Conference and the Parliamentary leaders were to persist for any length of time—ultimately either the Conference would win or the Party would split. A tree cannot survive unless sustained by its roots.

Yet such eventualities seem unlikely to develop. The Labour leadership normally wins support for its policies at Party Conferences. And the tradition of voting does not necessarily weaken the position of the leaders. True, it might encourage them to adjust policies to be more sure of obtaining a firm majority. Alternatively, if leaders are certain of victory, albeit by a narrow margin, they may be encouraged to adhere strictly to their views. Recent experience suggests that the latter probability is the more likely.

Argument within the Labour Party on policy is focused on the annual conferences. Because of the operation of the block vote, the crucial decisions may be made by trade unions before

[1] For fuller discussion of this topic see R. T. McKenzie, *British Political Parties* (Heinemann, 1955), and A. H. Birch, *Representative and Responsible Government* (Allen & Unwin, 1964), pp. 126–30.

125

the Conference meets or by trade union delegations at the Conference. In this process the Member of Parliament tends to be left on one side. But his voice is still of vital importance since it is the Parliamentary Party that chooses and sustains the Party Leader, and this can involve, as in 1960, defying the will of the Conference. Since Members have this power, one might expect them to be under substantial pressure from their constituency organizations at moments of high intra-party tension. In fact, when the Party was consumed by controversy over nuclear disarmament in 1960–1 there was little evidence that Members were greatly bothered by local supporters. A pro-Gaitskell organization, the Campaign for Democratic Socialism, was launched and secured the nomination of candidates favourable to its views in a few constituencies, but no attempts were made to oust sitting Members because of their views on the nuclear issue. Various reasons may be adduced for this inaction. The anti-nuclear decision at Scarborough was carried by the trade unions with a majority of constituency parties voting against in sympathy with Gaitskell:[1] this suggests that the greater number of Labour Members were not in conflict with their local supporters over the issue. No doubt, there was a general wish to avoid local squabbles that would split the Party even further. It is also the case that most Members have a fund of local respect and goodwill that is sufficient to protect their freedom of judgment on any matter that causes deep divisions among their adherents. Indeed, there is some evidence that pressure worked in the other way, i.e. that Members influenced their local organizations: constituency parties that voted for unilateralism in 1960 and changed their policy at the 1961 Conference had Members who supported Gaitskell.[2]

What conclusions can be drawn about the impact of the views of the Labour rank-and-file on foreign policy questions? Clearly, it is difficult for them to change the attitude of their parliamentary leaders. In the elections to the National Executive Committee of the Labour Party both Gordon Walker and Michael Stewart have been decisively defeated, but this did not prevent their subsequent appointments as Foreign Secretary.

[1] K. Hindell and P. Williams, 'Scarborough and Blackpool' in *Political Quarterly* (1962), Vol. 33, pp. 306–20.
[2] *Ibid.*, p. 315.

And recent events show that backbench Members are well insulated from local displeasure on foreign issues provided that they do not stray beyond the limits of party orthodoxy in the direction of their Conservative opponents. Intra-party democracy, in so far as it works at all, operates with a distinct bias in favour of the leadership.

The situation in the Conservative Party is different in both theory and atmosphere. The Party Conference merely advises on issues of policy: ultimate authority rests with the Leader. There is a reluctance to put questions to the vote, witness the 1965 Conference discussion on Rhodesia. There is also a great ability to conceal and blur differences. If Conservatives engage in less public argument among themselves than do Labour supporters, there is still substantial private discussion among opinion leaders within the Party. All these factors help to make attribution of influence difficult if not impossible. Differences among Conservatives on the ultimate objectives of foreign policy are rarely profound and this relative consensus, combined with the empirical character of Toryism, may mean that the Party leadership is more likely to adjust to constituency pressure. Nigel Nicolson in his account of the Suez crisis lays stress on the importance of the demand for strong action against Nasser by Conservatives at the 1956 Conference.[1] How far did this have influence on subsequent events? Were there any doubts in the Prime Minister's mind that were quelled by the bellicosity of the Conference? Rhodesia provides a clear example of constituency influence. After the Party split in the Commons over support for oil sanctions, local support for Members who opposed sanctions was quickly forthcoming. In order to unify the Party, Selwyn Lloyd was sent to Salisbury and subsequently the Party adopted the policy of urging 'talks' with the Smith regime. This incident suggests that the channels of communication within the Conservative Party may be more sensitive between Conferences than those of the Labour Party.

Clearly, both major parties are polyarchical in structure and the influence of each sector can never be defined precisely.

[1] *People and Parliament*, pp. 113–37. See also A. Husler, *Contribution à l'étude de l'élaboration de la politique étrangère britannique* (Librarie Droz, 1961), pp. 176–7.

PRESSURE GROUPS

Pressure group activity is less marked in foreign affairs than it is on domestic, economic and moral issues. Nevertheless it is not inconsiderable. Leading organizations in this sphere are the United Nations Association, various 'Peace' groups, the Campaign for Nuclear Disarmament and Amnesty International. There are also a number of associations designed to assist friendship and cultural relations with particular foreign countries; the promotion of this type of 'understanding' may well have political overtones as with the Society for Cultural Relations with the USSR. The Anglo-Rhodesian Society is a propagandist body: its prime purpose is 'to remedy the ignorance and dispel the prejudice' about Rhodesia. Some groups are relatively permanent; others, e.g. those pro and anti the Common Market, arise and fade in response to specific issues.

Organised attempts to arouse public feeling on international matters are relatively scarce because they do not affect the public so immediately as domestic problems. Distance generates apathy. It follows that few international questions create enough concern to cause the formation of pressure groups. Most of those that do exist are a product of East-West conflict and the consequent fear of war. Their motivation is primarily ethical. In contrast, interest groups dealing with home affairs frequently have material or selfish motives—apart from those excited by our moral welfare. Of course not all pressure groups in the international field are altruistic: the Anglo-Rhodesian Society is certainly interested in the prosperity of those who have invested capital in Rhodesia. This difference in motivation may also help to explain the relative disinterest in events overseas. Those who are affected by ethical questions may feel as deeply as those who are bothered about their own material welfare, but in terms of numbers the latter are almost always in a majority.

Pressure groups operate in different ways and at different levels on the hierarchy of public discussion. Some appeal for support to a mass audience; some concentrate on influential persons, the so-called opinion leaders. Members of Parliament are an obvious target for group activity. Parliamentary candidates all receive questionnaires from a variety of organizations asking for their views on particular topics. (A candidate standing for the first time and standing where his party is certain to win will attract much more attention than someone who has stood before and who is certain to lose). But relatively few of these enquiries relate to foreign policy although others may have implications concerning international trade. Candidates elected to the Commons receive a great deal of propaganda material through the post and pressure groups tend to concentrate, not unnaturally, on Members sympathetic to their point of view. Information supplied by these bodies sometimes becomes the basis of speeches in Parliament. Then a sympathetic Member can be asked to join a committee or become a Vice-President of an organization and become recognized as its parliamentary spokesman. Influence exerted through these links with Parliament is not necessarily one-way; parliamentarians may advise the organizations they support, especially on tactics. The United Nations Association has a Policy Committee which in 1965 consisted of five people—two had seats in the Commons, another was the wife of a Member and another was an ex-Member. The UNA is in a peculiarly strong position since it attracts support from all the main parties; one Labour Member and one Conservative were included on its Policy Committee. Its impact is limited, however, in so far as the message it spreads is non-controversial. Normally the idea of support for the United Nations and for the principle of international co-operation is broadly acceptable, but there have been occasions, notably Suez and the Congo, when United Nations' actions have been strongly opposed by some Conservatives.

The main organizations created to support and oppose the plan of the Macmillan Government to join the European Economic Community displayed a complete contrast in style and method of operation.[1] The Anti-Common Market League was a propagandist body holding public meetings throughout the country, recruiting a mass membership and giving general reinforcement to the opinions of the *Daily Express*. At first the League regarded itself as a Conservative organization but as membership grew it became clear that many supporters would not be associated with the Party. Subsequently, the Tory connexion was not stressed although Conservative Members

[1] Lord Windlesham, *Communication and Political Power* (Cape, 1966), Ch. 6.

were a main target of the League and some of them addressed its meetings. A vast amount of literature was distributed, 30,000 people joined the League and the intervention of an Anti-Common Market candidate in the South Dorset by-election of November, 1962, split the Conservative vote and presented a normally safe Tory seat to the Labour candidate. The rival national organization was the Common Market Campaign which started as an off-shoot of Federal Union.[1] A number of both Labour and Conservative Members took a prominent part in Campaign activities. (Its Labour adherents subsequently helped with the formation of a Labour Committee for Europe designed to work within the Labour Party, trade unions and the co-operative movement.) The Campaign addressed itself primarily to persons of authority and influence—especially Members of Parliament and industrialists. Many of the small-scale gatherings it arranged were held in the Palace of Westminster under the sponsorship of sympathetic Members. Few public meetings were held because the aim was to persuade an elite of opinion leaders rather than the general public. The contrast between the League and the Campaign reflects their basic diversity of purpose: the former had to stir up suspicion and hostility to Government policy among Government supporters, while the latter tried to spread specialized information that would promote fuller understanding and acceptance of the ministerial initiative. There was here also a curious reversal of roles. Usually right-wing pressure is exercised quietly in the corridors of power while radical orators strive to arouse the populace.

In recent years the outstanding example of a pressure group attempting to stir up political feeling has been the Campaign for Nuclear Disarmament.[2] Although essentially concerned with the morality of nuclear weapons, the CND programme inevitably had major implications for the nation's foreign policy. CND attracted its greatest strength from supporters of the Labour Party and it had much more influence upon the mass member-

[1] Federal Union was founded in 1938 as an all party organisation to advance the cause of world or regional government based on federal principles. Its interest in the Common Market was, therefore, political rather than economic.
[2] For a study of CND see C. Driver, *The Disarmers* (Hodder, 1964).

130

ship than on Party representatives in Parliament. The vote in favour of unilateralism at the 1960 Scarborough Conference had no parallel in the Parliamentary Labour Party. About seventy Labour Members in the Commons appear to have had some sympathy with CND, but this only equalled the usual size of the Left-wing of the Party in the nineteen-fifties: seventy Members supported Aneurin Bevan in the leadership election of 1955. This suggests that CND had little effect on Labour Members. Conversely, the Labour Party and its political prospects had a major effect on the Campaign. Labour Members supporting CND were gravely embarrassed by proposals that the movement should run its own parliamentary candidates, or that it should urge electors not to vote for any candidate who did not approve its policy. As a General Election became more imminent in 1963 with good prospects of a Labour victory, Labour Members ceased to play a prominent role in CND activities. Anthony Greenwood (Lab. Rossendale) resigned his Vice-Presidency. This was at a time when interest in the Campaign was fading and its leaders were dispirited by the success of the Campaign for Democratic Socialism that had led to the rejection of unilateralism at Blackpool in 1961.

Although there were some differences on tactics among the nuclear disarmers, their central aim was to capture the Labour Party. The argument was stated simply in the *New Statesman* (July 2, 1960) by Kingsley Martin: 'I know of no way of obtaining a non-nuclear Britain except by converting the Labour Party. Unless they work through the Labour movement, nuclear disarmers are simply marching about to satisfy their own consciences.' In Britain the main political parties are so firmly rooted in our political culture as to be irremovable by any new mass movement. When a new movement tries to work through a major party, it will find that if a clash of loyalty develops supporters of the party stick to the party and not to the pressure group. Thus in 1961 Michael Foot (Lab. Ebbw Vale), a leading CND supporter, said that he would not vote for a Conservative or Liberal unilateralist candidate against a Labour candidate who supported the Bomb.[1]

The Committee of 100—the extremist faction of nuclear

---

[1] *Ibid*, p. 70.

disarmers who advocated direct action—had perhaps rather more effect on parliamentary opinion in that they united all sections of the Labour Party in condemnation of illegal activities. In a debate on prison conditions Anthony Greenwood stressed that he 'was as much opposed to civil disobedience as anyone in this House'.[1]

A fairly recent development has been the use of public relations consultants by pressure groups. Firms are employed to get in touch with influential persons, including journalists and Members of Parliament, to persuade them of the validity of a particular viewpoint or, to use advertising jargon, to project a 'favourable image' of their clients. Activity of this nature has relevance to a study of foreign affairs since foreign governments have engaged the assistance of public relations operators in London.[2] The Central African Federation, Senegal, Katanga, Spain and Portugal have all utilised this technique. The best known example is the unsuccessful efforts of Voice and Vision on behalf of the Central African Federation. This firm is a subsidiary of Colman Prentis and Varley who have been used as P.R. consultants by the Conservative Party. It is notable that many of those who work in this specialized field have had previous connexions either with the Conservative Central Office or with public relations work in Government Departments. Clearly, knowing some of the right people and knowing the social patterns of Westminster, Whitehall and Fleet Street is an invaluable asset for this type of political persuasion. Commerical interests also make great use of public relations and in the case of East Germany the question of trade is indissolubly linked with world politics. The East German Chamber of Foreign Trade has used a public relations firm, Notley Ltd., to promote its interests in Britain. At least two Conservative Members have been associated with Notley Ltd. Visits of Members have been arranged to the Leipzig Trade Fair. There is no reason why Members should not promote—and profit from —the growth of international trade, but there is little doubt that the East German Government attempted to exploit these visits for political ends in the hope that development of trading

[1] H.C. Deb., Vol. 673, col. 1269.
[2] For fuller discussion of this topic see Ian Waller's article 'Pressure Politics' in *Encounter*, August, 1962, especially pp. 9–15.

relations might lead to pressure for political recognition.

Professional lobbying of politicians has attracted criticism, notably the arrangement of free trips abroad for Members and the use of dining facilities in the Palace of Westminster to provide hospitality for Members by private interests. Public expression of disquiet[1] may have helped to prevent abuses. But while slick public relations work is an unpleasant intrusion into public life, there is no prospect of it being able to affect the pattern of our foreign policy.

PARLIAMENTARY PRESSURES

Both the major parties arrange regular meetings of their parliamentary supporters at which backbench opinion can be ventilated. Conservatives in the Commons attend meetings of what is known as the 1922 Committee: the corresponding Labour organization, the Parliamentary Labour Party, is open also to Labour Peers. General meetings are supplemented by the creation of Groups specializing in particular topics, including, of course, one on foreign affairs.[2] There are also inter-party committees concerned to press a particular viewpoint, e.g. the Parliamentary Group for World Government and the United Nations Parliamentary Group.

The more important Conservative committees meet weekly. Sometimes the Foreign Affairs Group has a speaker and sometimes there is a general discussion of policy among Members. In the past this Group appears to have had little influence, largely because Conservatives do not normally suffer the deep divisions on foreign policy which often split the Labour Party. Consequently Tory backbenchers tend to rest content with the attitudes adopted by their leaders. But in 1966 there were thinly veiled disputes among Conservative leaders over foreign and defence policy. One school of thought led by Sir Alec Douglas-Home was that Britain should honour to the full her widespread international obligations and force herself to afford the scale of armed forces necessary to do so. The other view associated with

[1] E.g. by Edward Heath, Lord Privy Seal, in March, 1962, H.C. Deb., Vol. 656, cols. 28–9, and Harold Wilson, Leader of the Opposition in April, 1963, H.C. Deb., Vol. 676, col. 412.

[2] For a general description of the work of party committees see Peter G. Richards, *Honourable Members* (Faber, 1964), pp. 97–109.

133

Enoch Powell was that Britain should recognise that her interests were essentially European and that the nation's defence commitments must have a realistic relationship to our economic resources. The clash of opinion centred on the British role in Asia: how far should we seek to retain influence in this area by maintaining bases there? The policy presented to the 1966 Conservative Conference envisaged the continued presence of British air forces in Asia but perhaps not of ground troops. This compromise formula, according to *The Guardian*,[1] was hammered out at several joint meetings of the Foreign Affairs Group and the Defence Group. The Commonwealth Affairs Group was a focus for backbench pressure, supplemented by constituency pressure, which forced a slow change in Conservative policy on Rhodesia. It is significant that the Conservatives tended to treat this problem as one of colonial independence, not of foreign affairs, and so rather ignored its international implications.

Conservative backbench committees have the greatest scope for activity when the Party is in opposition and counsels are divided. But whenever there is a split in Conservative opinion an informal group of Members may assemble which represents the minority view. In 1954 the decision to evacuate the Suez Canal zone was opposed by Right-wing Members who became known as the Suez Group. In 1956 some liberal-minded Conservatives opposed the invasion of the Canal Zone. United Nations' action against Katanga was opposed by a 'Congo Lobby' and a similar collection of Right-wingers urged that no sanctions be imposed against Rhodesia.

The Labour Foreign Affairs Group operates in a similar way to the corresponding Conservative Group. However, Labour Peers can join as of right, not by invitation; in practice, only a few come to meetings. The intensity of Group activity varies with changing circumstances but meetings are usually held about every three weeks. They are not held more often because of the pressure of other engagements upon Members' time. Attendance at a Group meeting varies widely between a dozen and a hundred or more depending on the nature of the business. Sometimes they have a guest speaker from outside Parliament.

[1] October 18, 1966.

When Labour is in power the Foreign Secretary, or another Foreign Office Minister, will talk to the Group from time to time to explain and defend his actions—these occasions attract the biggest audience. In opposition, the 'Shadow' Foreign Secretary is chairman of the Group: in office, a backbench chairman is elected. 1964 saw a clash between the Left and Right wings of the Party which produced a triangular contest for the Chairmanship and ended in victory for the Centre or compromise candidate. On the first ballot John Hynd (Sheffield, Attercliffe), representing the Right, obtained twenty-four votes, Philip Noel-Baker (Derby, South) had fifteen votes and the Left-wing John Mendelson (Penistone) had twelve supporters: on the second ballot, with Mendelson eliminated, Noel-Baker had a clear majority. The vigour of the contest and the publication of the result in the Press are both highly significant. Theoretically the business of all party meetings is confidential; but the accounts of the larger and more exciting ones are published regularly. These 'leaks' are impossible to stop in the case of large meetings. Small gatherings remain effectively secret because of the greater possibility of tracing informants.[1] These leaks have an effect on the proceedings of the Foreign Affairs Group: because privacy is not assumed any Minister must be guarded in his statements and his speech may be little more frank or revealing than a parallel speech in the Chamber. The size of the gathering also precludes the type of intimacy that develops between some Ministers and their corresponding backbench committees. Further, Left-wing Labour Members appear to concentrate their energies on the Foreign Affairs Group so that the pattern of discussion at its meetings does not necessarily reflect the balance of opinion in the Parliamentary Labour Party as a whole. A tradition of tension has almost developed between a Labour Foreign Secretary and the Foreign Affairs Group—Bevin's relations with the Group were strained and the same was true of Stewart.

In the 1964 Parliament the Foreign Affairs Group instituted an executive or steering committee to plan its meetings. This

[1] The Committee of Privileges decided in 1947 that to betray information about private party gatherings was not a breach of privilege, but to receive payment for such information was a contempt of the House. See its report on the Allighan Case: 1946–7 (138) ix.

meant that the usual officers, Chairman, Vice-Chairman, Secretary and Treasurer, could be supplemented by a few other Members to ensure that all sections of party opinion were represented on a steering committee. It is possible, although unlikely, that this committee will increase the effectiveness of the Foreign Affairs Group in influencing policy. In January, 1966, the committee met the Prime Minister to express the disquiet among Labour Members for British support for the resumption of American bombing in North Vietnam. But this was exceptional. No doubt a Labour Foreign Secretary would always agree to meet this committee but it has no right of audience with the Prime Minister. Looking at the record one is forced to conclude that the Foreign Affairs Group has had little impact on the foreign policy of Labour Governments.[1] It is possible that the Foreign Secretary's public dissent in Washington over the use of gas in Vietnam was stimulated by a cable of protest from Labour Members. Otherwise on Vietnam Stewart seemed to have budged not at all.

In addition to the Foreign Affairs Group there are other collections of Labour Members, formal and informal, created to press a particular policy or to concentrate on a particular aspect of foreign affairs. The two formal groups, the Labour Committee for Europe and the Wider Europe Group, symbolize the differences of view within the Labour Party on the issue of European integration. The Committee for Europe is broadly in favour of joining the Common Market on acceptable terms: the Wider Europe Group asserts the need for closer association with all the countries of Europe. However, the distinction of attitude is not wholly clearcut since a few supporters of the Wider Europe Group are not necessarily averse to joining the Common Market and argue that such action would not be incompatible with closer ties with the whole of the Continent. These two organizations differ in composition. The Wider Europe Group is exclusively parliamentary: the Committee for Europe includes Labour sympathizers outside Parliament who may be asked to join if it is thought they have specialized knowledge or may be otherwise useful, e.g. economists and trade unionists. Both organizations are formal in the sense that they appoint officers

---

[1] A final assessment of backbench influence is in Chapter IX.

and have regular meetings but are unofficial in that they are not part of the activities of the Parliamentary Labour Party.

The PLP agreed in November, 1966, that all unofficial groups of Labour Members must be notified to the Chief Whip and be accepted by him as compatible with Party purposes. This move was an attempt to outlaw gatherings of critics of Government policy. Private groups had long been a source of trouble. In 1965 opponents of entry to the Common Market made an unsuccessful attempt to get the Whips to ban the Labour Committee for Europe on the ground that it constituted a 'party within the Party'. In November, 1952, the Parliamentary Labour Party condemned meetings of the Left-wing supporters of Aneurin Bevan on this precise formula and the Bevanite meetings were discontinued. The Committee for Europe survived the challenge presumably because it was not thought to be a basic threat to Party policy or leadership. It is certainly true that the aim of these groups is to try to push Labour policy in a particular direction. This is done by canvassing for support among Labour Members, by discussion with Foreign Office Ministers and with other Ministers known to be sympathetic who may advise on tactics. The Committee for Europe arranges some educational activities and meetings with socialists from Common Market countries: although little publicised, its activities have been highly influential.

Informal groups, now theoretically prohibited, have no officers and no regular meetings. They consist of like-minded Members concerned with particular issues who tend to gather together when they feel that some collective action may be useful. One such group of Labour Members sent letters to *The Times* about Rhodesia. The largest body consists of the Left-wingers who are constantly critical of American policy.[1] In the 1964–6 Parliament they used a variety of means in attempts to influence events. As already noted, the Left-wingers tended to dominate discussion at the Foreign Affairs Group; they sent

[1] Many of these are associated with the Labour Peace Fellowship, whose Chairman is Frank Allaun (Salford, East). Any individual who belongs to the Labour Party can join this body and trade union organizations can affiliate to it. The L.P.F. is essentially a pressure group within the Labour Party. It is not pacifist but favours cuts in defence expenditure and urges the need for peaceful co-existence.

letters to the Prime Minister; they put down motions on the Commons' Order Paper; they got in touch with opponents of the Vietnam war in the United States. This last technique—the international initiative—was the most spectacular for at the end of January, 1966, no fewer than 96 Members, 92 Labour and 4 Liberal, sent a cable to Senator Fulbright asking him and other members of Congress to continue to oppose the extension of the cruel and dangerous war in Vietnam. An earlier international foray by backbenchers ended in disciplinary action. In April, 1948, a number of Labour Members signed a telegram of support for Signor Nenni, leader of the Left-wing group of Italian Socialists who were fighting the Italian election in alliance with the Communists but in competition with the Right-wing or orthodox democratic Socialists. The Whip was subsequently withdrawn from the instigator of the telegram, J. Platts-Mills (Finsbury).

The most usual outcome of pressure on backbenchers and of discontent amongst them is the appearance of a motion on the Order Paper. Known as Early Day Motions because they are put down for debate 'on an early day', they are rarely discussed since no time is made available for their consideration. Discussion could arise only if a Member successful in the ballot for private members' motions happened to adopt an Early Day Motion. But they do provide an excellent opportunity of ventilating opinions and are blessed with procedural advantages. A motion can be put down at any time during the session so the response to an important development in international affairs can be immediate and need not await the next debate on foreign policy. Since Members usually sponsor motions as a group initiative and can add their names after a motion has been tabled, the procedure allows for aggregation of support and more Members demonstrate their opinions than can ever be called on to speak in debate. Further, and this is the vital aspect, these motions are not subject to control by the party Whips. As a matter of courtesy, a Member should inform his Whip when he is promoting a motion, and the latter may attempt to dissuade the Member from taking action that would cause his party embarrassment. However, it is accepted that Members do as they wish in relation to motions: disciplinary powers are invoked solely for indiscipline in the division lobbies. So motions provide an avenue of freedom for backbenchers who, especially in the Labour Party, make considerable use of the facility.[1]

Motions are peculiarly valuable as indicators of political opinion where a party is split on an important issue. If one wing or group in a party put down a motion on a topic of controversy within the party, another group from the same party may come forward with an amendment or another motion that expresses a different viewpoint. This can lead to 'a battle of the Order Paper' among supporters of one party. Motions may, of course, be signed by Members from more than one party. It is also possible, if unusual, for them to be sponsored by party leaders: in 1965 the leaders of all three parties initiated a motion expressing support for the Governor of Rhodesia, Sir Humphrey Gibbs.

Other examples illustrate the importance of this procedure on matters of controversy. After the Suez debacle anti-American feeling in the Conservative policy was strong; 127 Conservative Members signed a motion that asserted the attitude of the United States was 'gravely endangering the Atlantic alliance'.[2] Subsequently a number of anti-American incidents were reported in this country and an all-party motion deploring these incidents was supported by 17 Conservatives and 97 Labour Members. In February, 1959, 37 Labour Members tabled a motion on the German problem urging the *de facto* recognition of the East German Government, a suggestion not included in official Party policy. Over a hundred Labour Members then supported a rival motion that stressed the need for re-unification of Germany under a free Government. Finally a rather un-

[1] Another procedure, rarely used, is to ask for the appointment of a Select Committee. In November, 1965, three Labour Members, Frank Allaun (Salford, East), Sydney Silverman (Nelson and Colne) and William Warbey (Ashfield) signed a motion asking that a Committee 'enquire into the circumstances that caused Her Majesty's Ministers to be misled into informing the House and the British Public that the Government of the Democratic Republic of North Vietnam and of the Chinese People's Republic were solely responsible for the breakdown of all efforts during 1964 and 1965 to bring about negotiations for a settlement of the conflict in Vietnam'.

[2] The maximum of signatories to the motion at any time was 118 as some Members repented and removed their names while other Members added theirs: Leon D. Epstein, *British Politics in the Suez Crisis* (Pall Mall, 1964), p. 57f.

successful attempt was made to get general acceptance of a compromise motion.[1] At a critical stage in the Common Market negotiations, in December, 1962, 47 Conservatives tabled a motion that showed anxiety over the Cabinet's eagerness to join Europe. Another case of a demonstration by Government backbenchers against Government policy was the motion in March, 1965, signed by 55 Labour Members which argued that there should be no identity of view between the British and United States Governments over Vietnam. This stimulated Emanuel Shinwell, the octogenarian chairman of the Parliamentary Labour Party, to produce a 'unity' motion calling for an end to the fighting in Vietnam which all shades of opinion in the Party might support. The examples can be multiplied, but it will be apparent that any important development in politicians' views on foreign policy is likely to be echoed on the Commons' Order Paper.

Bare numbers of supporters are a poor guide to the significance of a motion. Some are canvassed more vigorously than others. Some are worded ambiguously to attract more adherents. Some Members are always willing to sign if they are broadly in sympathy with what appears to them to be the purpose of a motion: other Members are more cautious. Thus support should be measured in qualitative as well as quantitative terms. A Conservative motion sponsored solely by adherents of the Monday Club will have much less impact than one backed by middle-of-the-party knights of the shires. Equally, a move by the regular Labour Left-wingers can be less easily discounted should it be sustained by a cross-section of the Party. One distinction should be made here. On domestic issues the most significant motions often emanate from government backbenches. With foreign policy this is not necessarily true since a motion may reveal cracks in a broad pattern of agreement between Government and Opposition.

An Early Day Motion is an orthodox and somewhat subdued form of parliamentary protest. Backbench amendments to the Speech from the Throne are similar in effect since they are never called by the Speaker, but they do attract more publicity. In 1946 a hundred Labour Members tabled such an amendment

---

[1] S. E. Finer, H. B. Berrington, D. J. Bartholomew, *Backbench Opinion in the House of Commons 1955–59* (Pergamon Press, 1961), pp. 168–72.

criticising the subservience of the Labour Government to the United States. In 1966 two groups of backbenchers put down amendments. Thirty-two Labour Members regretted the absence of any reference in the Gracious Speech to the dangerous intensification of the Vietnam war, while six Right-wing Conservatives deplored the lack of any mention of the urgent need to initiate talks with Rhodesia.

The most vigorous and direct forms of backbench protest by-pass the Order Paper completely. Deputations are sent to lobby Foreign Office ministers. More than once Left-wing Labour Members have sent a collective letter to Prime Minister Wilson about Vietnam. A yet more drastic step is resignation: in February, 1965, Frank Allaun resigned his post as parliamentary private secretary[1] to the Colonial Secretary also due to dissatisfaction with the official attitude over Vietnam. Two Junior Ministers, Sir Edward Boyle and Anthony Nutting, resigned office in protest against the invasion of Suez. A Conservative Member may resign the whip, i.e. voluntarily withdraw from the parliamentary party, as an expression of hostility to some aspect of policy. Thus in May, 1957, eight Conservatives forsook the whip because they felt that the Macmillan Government had 'capitulated to Nasser' by allowing British ships to again use the Suez Canal. In December, 1966, Reginald Paget (Lab. Northampton) resigned the whip as a prelude to voting against the Government's Rhodesia policy. Labour left-wingers are not in the habit of giving up the whip, but it may be withdrawn from them should they vote against party policy. To fail to support his party in the division lobby is the ultimate form of protest for a backbencher. Such action may be caused by high principle or despair and, as has been shown above, the consequences of rebellion for an individual Member are serious.

The only 'free vote' in Parliament on foreign affairs would be that in a party meeting which means, in effect, at a meeting of the Parliamentary Labour Party, since the Conservatives avoid votes. Even this vote is not wholly free because when Labour is in power the Ministers, Whips and even the Parliamentary Private Secretaries will be expected to support the leadership.

---

[1] A parliamentary private secretary is an unpaid assistant to a minister who acts as a parliamentary liaison officer. He is not a member of the Government but is expected to support Government policies.

At present, including the Whips, there are 110 members of the Government who together with another forty or so P.P.S.s can virtually ensure that a Labour Cabinet will always command a majority at a Party meeting.[1] With a smaller number of Ministers than there are to-day the Attlee Government easily survived challenges by vote at PLP meetings. When Labour is in Opposition, the outcome is little different. The established Right-wing view secures a majority unless the Right-wing position is itself changing. After the failure of the Berlin Conference in February, 1954, the PLP accepted the idea of a German contribution to Western defence by the narrow margin of 113 to 104: a motion by Harold Wilson that the possibilities of negotiation with the Soviet Union were not exhausted and that German rearmament be not supported was defeated by 111 to 109.[2] In the 1964–6 Parliament no votes were demanded at Party meetings because any overt demonstration of disunity might have done irreparable damage to the authority of the Government with its tiny majority in the Commons. However, in June, 1966, a vote was forced on the Government's East-of-Suez policy and the dissidents were defeated by 225 to 54. In the absence of official division lists it is impossible to give an accurate analysis of how the voting went. One does not know how many Peers were present and how many of those present abstained. There appears to have been a large attendance of senior and junior Ministers, so the Commons' backbenchers probably supported Government policy by a majority of less than two to one. In July, 1966, a challenge on Vietnam policy was defeated in the PLP by 214 to 46 after the Government had dissociated itself from American bombing of Hanoi and Haiphong. Next day thirty-two Members abstained at a division in the Chamber on the same issue. On these occasions the Left-wing critics were split, some feeling that the Prime Minister's criticism of American actions entitled him to their support.

Is it good tactics for critics within the PLP to challenge votes on foreign policy? Any vote probably overestimates the support the Ministers have. Partly this is because some Members are

[1] For fuller discussion of the patronage powers of the Prime Minister see Peter G. Richards, *Patronage in British Government* (Allen & Unwin, 1963, Toronto: University of Toronto Press), especially Ch. 4.

[2] D. C. Watt, *Britain Looks to Germany* (Oswald Woolf, 1965), p. 126.

loath to declare themselves formally against Government policy and partly it is due to the substantial advantages that Party leaders enjoy in any direct confrontation. The Prime Minister will be allowed a much longer time to speak than any one of his critics and he may with skill deflect the centre of attention by emphasising those aspects of Government policy which enjoy full support in the Party. Thus at the June, 1966, meeting Prime Minister Harold Wilson stressed support for the United Nations and the need for this country to take a full share of the task of world peace-keeping. If the pattern of proceedings were altered, if the Party leadership were subjected to interrogation before the vote, then issues could be clarified more effectively and the outcome might be somewhat different. As it is, pressure on Ministers may be more potent when a vote is avoided, for an impression can be created of major, if unmeasured, dissatisfaction with Government policy. Ministers may then feel that something should be done to alleviate discontent; the support gained from a decisive majority vote can lead to a feeling that criticism can safely be disregarded.

CHAPTER VIII

A Parliamentary Committee for Foreign Affairs?

OVER the past sixty years a large number of writers have advocated the establishment of specialized parliamentary committees. Details of the proposals have varied and there has been an assortment of ideas about the function, constitution and *modus operandi* of the committees. But all these schemes stem from a common belief that Parliament, as at present organized, lacks both the information and opportunities necessary to enable it to carry out any effective review of the activities of Government Departments. Some writers have urged that a group of committees be created which would between them cover all Government action; others have put forward the particular need for a committee to specialize on foreign affairs. It would be tedious to recall details of all these plans especially when on close examination some prove to be not wholly clear. But an amount of description is necessary to show how these ideas have evolved.

Fred Jowett, for many years Labour Member for Bradford, produced a scheme in 1907 which involved the nomination of a separate Commons' committee to supervise each Government Department. These committees were intended to function like those in local government: each Minister would be Chairman of the committee concerned with his Department and it would examine all legislative and administrative matters within its scope before they were discussed by the whole House. Departmental documents should be available to these bodies. This municipalization scheme was clearly inappropriate to the business of central government and it helped to discredit subsequent and more sophisticated plans for specialized committees. Another factor which restricted the impact of these ideas was that, at least until after the Second World War, their advocates tended to be of Left-wing opinions—Ramsay Mac-Donald,[1] Harold Laski,[2] Ramsay Muir,[3] Lloyd George[4] and W. Ivor Jennings.[5]

The proposal for a Foreign Affairs Committee of Parliament has attracted support from a further group of writers who were not necessarily concerned with wider schemes of institutional reform. Their general argument has been that the special character of foreign relations, especially the need for secrecy, renders largely inoperable the normal processes of parliamentary control. As early as 1908 Sir Sidney Low urged the establishment of such a body drawn from both Houses of Parliament which would meet *in camera* and have power to call for documents and drafts of treaties with foreign states. Its functions would be advisory but, owing to the veil of secrecy, the public would not know how far the Cabinet had acted on its advice. Even so, Sir Sidney felt that the country would have more confidence in the Foreign Office if it knew that its work were being investigated in this manner.[6] Arthur Ponsonby, the advocate of open diplomacy, necessarily wanted a different type of committee. His plan was for a deliberative and representative body, containing from thirty to fifty Members of the Commons, which might be used to bring popular pressure to bear on the Foreign Secretary.[7] Viscount Bryce[8] felt that the experiment of a Foreign Affairs Committee should be tried and H. R. G. Greaves argued the case for it in detail in a Fabian pamphlet.[9] Greaves' plan was for a body of twenty-five Members selected in proportion to party strength in the Commons which could make reports to the House, co-opt additional Members, make decisions by vote and have power to meet during parliamentary recesses. The proceedings would not be secret and thus avoid the prospect of breaches

---

[1] *Parliament and Revolution* (National Labour Press, 1919), Appendix.

[2] *Grammar of Politics* (Allen & Unwin, 1925), pp. 349–50.

[3] *How Britain is Governed* (Constable, 1930).

[4] Evidence to the Select Committee on Procedure, 1930–1. HC. 161, pp. 349–561, viii.

[5] *Parliamentary Reform* (Gollancz, 1934), Ch. IX.

[6] *The Governance of England* (T. Fisher Unwin), pp. 299–305.

[7] *Democracy and Diplomacy* (Methuen, 1915), Ch. VIII.

[8] *Modern Democracies* (Macmillan, 1921), Vol. II, p. 420.

[9] *Parliamentary Control of Foreign Affairs* (N.F.R.B., 1934).

of confidence. The Foreign Secretary would not be compelled to answer questions raised by the committee, but if he did not, or if he were evasive, then this would be noticed. Greaves argued that this plan would save time in the whole House, and it should be useful for a Foreign Secretary to try out his ideas on a small committee. It was important that the quality of membership should be high and it would generally include some ex-Foreign Office Ministers.

To revert to more general schemes for specialized committees, the best known has been that of Harold J. Laski, first set out in his *Grammar of Politics* (1925) and repeated, with minor variations, in *Parliamentary Government in England* (1938)[1] and *Reflections on the Constitution* (1951).[2] Laski urged that the Commons should establish a separate committee to watch over each Government Department. They would have power to initiate enquiries, to hear evidence from civil servants and have access to all papers 'save those of an especially confidential kind'. They would have regular meetings with the Minister when his policy would be discussed. The committees would not be policy makers, but they would have an advisory role and would bring to the legislature 'a definitely competent opinion upon the working of the administrative process'. Laski's plan was sometimes discussed in academic circles, and it received support from people not associated with Left-wing thought,[3] but it was not until the nineteen sixties that the creation of such committees began to seem a practical possibility.

Interest in procedural reform in the Commons was revitalized by the Select Committee on Procedure in 1958, the appointment of which was a direct consequence of backbench dissatisfaction with the pattern of parliamentary business. Hanson and Wiseman of Leeds University urged the Committee to adopt the Laski plan of committees.[4] In 1959 Bernard Crick produced a Fabian pamphlet on the same theme which subsequently developed into a longer study *The Reform of Parliament*.[5] But

[1] Allen and Unwin.   [2] Manchester University Press.

[3] For example, G. M. Young and Lord Salter in *Parliament: A Survey* edited by Lord Campion (Allen and Unwin, 1952), pp. 118 and 281.

[4] Their memorandum to the Procedure Committee was subsequently published in *Public Law* (1959), pp. 272–92.

[5] Weidenfeld and Nicolson, 1964.

the 1958 Procedure Committee issued a conservative-minded
report which proposed a minimum of change.[1] Not only was the
idea of specialized committees brushed aside, but it rejected also
a proposal from Leslie Hale (Lab. Oldham, West) that a
committee be established to debate colonial affairs on the same
lines as the Scottish Grand Committee. However, the Procedure
Committee of 1964 was bolder: it recommended that the work of
the existing Estimates Committee be developed by a new
Select Committee working through sub-committees that could
concentrate on a particular aspect of public administration, e.g.
the social services.[2] The 1964 Committee had received evidence[3]
from a small newly created body of political scientists and members of the parliamentary staff known as the Study of Parliament
Group whose suggestions clearly had some influence, perhaps
because they were cautious. While the Group advocated specialized committees on the Laski model, it suggested that they
should scrutinize the administration of less controversial topics,
and so excluded defence and foreign affairs. This is a complete
change of emphasis from Low and Ponsonby who half-a-century
earlier were insisting that foreign affairs had particular need
of a parliamentary committee because of its confidential nature.

Proposals to establish specialized committees have always
encountered strong opposition. The standard objection is that
they would interfere with the operation of ministerial responsibility. Committees, it is said, would attempt to interfere
with the ministerial function of policy formulation. Alternatively, it is argued that Ministers must be responsible for policy
to the Commons as a whole and not to any section of it since a
small gathering may not be representative of the opinions of all
Members. Also we are warned to beware of the experience of
committee behaviour in the legislatures of France and the
United States.[4] Up to now the orthodox doctrine has been that
parliamentary committees should discuss questions of detail and
administration, not matters of general policy. In practice, this
distinction is breaking down. Although the Estimates Committee is instructed to 'recommend economies consistent with

[1] 1958–9 (92) vi.   [2] Fourth Report. 1964–5 (303) para. 10.
[3] *Ibid.*, pp. 131–42.
[4] Lord Morrison, *Government and Parliament* (O.U.P., 1954), pp.
155–6.

the policies implied in the Estimates', many observers feel that it sometimes crosses the indistinct boundary between policy and administration. Why should a committee not interest itself with policy? If it makes suggestions that a Minister finds unacceptable—then the Minister must reject them. So long as a committee has only advisory functions, no adverse vote by a committee has any legal effect. The 1958 Procedure Committee rejected the Hale Scheme for a Colonial Committee because 'There is little doubt that the activities of such a committee would ultimately be aimed at controlling rather than criticising the policy and the actions of the department concerned'.[1] This comment was absurd. A debating body, as envisaged by the Hale Scheme, could have neither the power nor the resources to supplant the executive in the slightest degree. Its deliberations might influence the Colonial Secretary in the same way that debate in the Commons' Chamber may influence Ministers, but in this sense all criticism is an attempt to control. If we end all criticism, we end Parliament.

The truth is that Ministers in the past have objected to specialized committees not really because of constitutional theory, but because they might cause embarrassment. A hostile committee, albeit with only advisory functions, could put pressure on a Minister that it would be more comfortable for him to avoid. Well informed committeemen, led by an able chairman, could produce more concentrated and damaging criticism than a diffuse debate in the House. A Minister supported by the Whips can always win a vote if his policy is challenged in the division lobbies; but Ministers do not want to govern by appeals to party discipline, they want to govern with popularity and a reputation for wisdom. Labour Foreign Secretaries are commonly at odds with the unofficial party committee on foreign affairs. How much more troublesome would these backbench critics be if this committee achieved official status and were joined by Opposition Members?

Yet specialist committees are not to be supported merely because Ministers have objected to them! There are two further arguments to be considered. The first is that backbenchers have not the time available to serve on extra committees. It is tempting to reply that specialized committees could largely replace

[1] 1958–9 (92) vi. para. 47.

the existing unofficial party groups, so that no additional burden would be placed on Members. But official committees are limited in numbers and nominations are arranged to secure a party representation proportionate to that in the whole House, whereas any Member can attend unofficial meetings of his own party. Thus if the establishment of an official Foreign Affairs Committee caused the emasculation of party foreign affairs groups, there must be a reduction in the number of Members taking an active interest in international problems. If official and unofficial bodies operate side by side, there must be some duplication of discussion and additional calls on Members' time. One suggestion to meet this situation is that civil servants might appear before party committees. Would this remove the desire for more information through specialized committees, thus avoiding repetition of discussion and other difficulties too? Certainly, if civil servants talk with Members more often, there should be benefit to both sides. But this new avenue for party committee activity would not meet the case of those who hold that the Commons as a democratic forum should have sufficient formal means to enable it to discover what the executive is doing and why it acts as it does.

The second difficulty is that no one can foretell with certainty exactly how these committees would operate in practice. Suppose a Minister manages to persuade a committee of the advantages of a new policy which later proves to be a disastrous failure—would it not be difficult to acquit the committee of a share of the blame? Could the Minister shuffle out of some of the responsibility and avoid censure? In the words of Professor Wheare, committees may be buffers or duffers. If relations between a Minister and his committee were too smooth, it might develop into a cosy little gathering giving general support to Government policy and seem rather set apart from the normal cut-and-thrust of the parliamentary struggle. This possibility would be enhanced wherever a committee is given access to 'inside' information and is, therefore, greatest in the spheres of defence and foreign affairs. It is significant that the leading Labour backbench critic of the Government's foreign policy, Jack Mendelson (Penistone), is also opposed to the idea of specialized committees.[1]

[1] H.C. Deb., Vol. 718, cols. 240–8.

149

There is one British precedent in this field—the Standing Joint Committee on Indian Affairs which arose out of a recommendation in the Montagu-Chelmsford Report.[1] This body was first nominated in 1921 and was empowered to examine any Bill or other matter referred to it by Parliament and to consider any matter raised by the Secretary of State for India or any committee member. Ministers were informed in confidence of items to be discussed. Ministers were invited to communicate with the committee which had the right to call for documentary and oral evidence. The Committee published reports but not the evidence it received. Appointed annually from 1921 to 1929, it failed to meet after 1925. It appears to have considered only four topics, a draft constitution for Burma, a Bill affecting the status of Indian civil servants, the cost of the Indian Army, and the position of the Indian community in Kenya. The last item produced unsuccessful protests that the Committee was exceeding its terms of reference.[2] But if this is a disappointing precedent for advocates of reform—it is also no guide to how specialized committees would work now. The pattern of parliamentary life in 1921 was very different from that of today. Equally, arguments by analogy about committee conduct in the United States, Germany or France are unconvincing because of the difference of constitutional structure and political tradition.

The behaviour of a future British Parliamentary Foreign Affairs Committee would depend on the conditions of its operation—membership, powers, relations with the Foreign Secretary, control of agenda, access to confidential material, etc. While permutations of detail are endless, basically there are three main possible types of arrangement—a debating committee, an investigating committee and a body meeting behind closed doors.

A debating committee offers few advantages. More time would be available for formal backbench discussion, and topics of secondary importance that now are overlooked might get some attention. But backbenchers would not obtain more information and the proceedings might not have much more effect than present debates in the Chamber.

The vital issue is whether the committee should work in

[1] 1918 Cd. 9109, para. 295 viii.
[2] 1921 (186) vi; 1922 (136) v; 1925 (127) vii.

secret and have access to confidential information, on the lines of the Foreign Affairs Committee of the West German Bundestag. Certainly there is no enthusiasm in high places for such meetings behind closed doors: the idea was rejected by both the Prime Minister and the Leader of the Opposition in 1958.[1] The main objection is that members of this private conclave would be unable to use all their knowledge should they wish to criticise Government policy and that this restraint would be highly frustrating and induce a sense of separation from their parliamentary colleagues. The same considerations apply to the question of whether there should be regular confidential discussions between Ministers and few prominent members of the Shadow Cabinet. Such talks on an informal *ad hoc* basis are now held intermittently, at the initiative of either side. But should they become an accepted part of constitutional practice, so that it could generally be assumed that Opposition leaders were fully appraised of the factual basis for Government policies? Confidential discussions are usually thought of in relation to the technicalities of defence rather than broad issues of foreign affairs, but on some matters, like Britain's nuclear capability and the structure of the NATO alliance, defence and foreign policy become inseparable.

In 1949 three confidential meetings were held between Government and Opposition leaders to discuss a memorandum prepared by Churchill on his view of Britain's unpreparedness for future war. Thereafter Churchill terminated the discussions as he felt they might inhibit public criticism of the Government. Subsequent leaders of the Opposition, Attlee and Gaitskell, turned down the idea of confidential talks and in 1966 the Conservative Opposition has avoided them. Wilson has been the only Opposition Leader of recent years to favour these private discussions; in the course of a Commons' speech in January, 1964, he urged that they be arranged. Nothing appears to have come of this proposal. Exactly why has never been made clear.[2]

[1] H.C. Deb., Vol. 586, cols. 1160-6.
[2] H.C. Deb., Vol. 687, col. 446 and Vol. 704, cols. 440-1. It is arguable that Wilson was in a peculiarly favourable political position at this time, which explains the difference of attitude. His expectation of becoming Prime Minister was obviously high and there was a clear difference between Government and Opposition on defence policy—over the 'independent' deterrent—that was unlikely to be affected by confidential discussions.

Usually, however, Opposition leaders feel that the possession of inside information may put them at a tactical disadvantage in the continuing domestic battle between political parties. To have material that must not be used in public argument is obviously frustrating for politicians. Even worse it may drive a wedge between them and their followers, who can easily become impatient and suspicious when they feel their own front-bench to be hesitant in its criticism of the Government. By reducing the size of his Shadow Government in 1966, Heath has tried to minimise the sense of division between leaders and led amongst Conservative Members; this sense of unity would be damaged if a few members of the Shadow Cabinet had regular consultations in Downing Street.

Are Opposition leaders entitled to condemn themselves to partial ignorance, to avoid knowing facts that Ministers are willing to place before them? Has the Opposition a higher duty than the duty to oppose? Professor Beloff thinks it has. In an article in *The Times*[1] he argued that 'All Members of Parliament ... are also obliged to serve the Crown and hence the national interest to the best of their abilities. To refuse information which might help them better to discharge their duties, particularly their duties with regard to the enlightening of public opinion seems to be conduct very doubtfully capable of being reconciled with such obligations'. His phraseology suggests a rather antique and idealized view of the working of British democracy. In realistic terms what does duty 'to serve the Crown' involve? No doubt, Members of Parliament would agree that they have a responsibility to assist the national interest—provided it be agreed that they judge the nature of the national interest. And since Parliament is now dominated by party loyalty, Members will feel that the national interest is best served if their own party is successful. Thus they become unwilling to admit any possible cleavage between party interest and national interest. The harsh fact is that if Opposition leaders think that confidential talks with the Government will be of use to them, they will favour them; otherwise, they will not.

A fair case can be made for asserting that politicians should not behave in this way—without invoking the concept of loyalty

---

[1] April 29, 1958.

to the Crown. Political controversy may well become unrealistic
in any field where the Opposition are deprived of essential
factual material. Further, if an Opposition is elected to office in
ignorance of the true situation, they may well be forced to adopt
policies which diverge from those which they had advocated
previously, thus provoking charges of cynical and dishonest
betrayal of electoral promises.

Yet there is another side to the picture which affects both
consultations between Government and Opposition leaders and
the idea of a Parliamentary Foreign Affairs Committee meeting
in secret. Might not public argument on foreign policy and
defence be stifled? Could not a synthetic consensus develop
based on a conspiracy of silence, perhaps disturbed by a few
voices, easily condemned as extremist and irresponsible because
they did not know the facts? Whitehall already places too high a
value on discretion. To quote Kenneth Younger: 'It is notorious
among backbench politicians that they can often acquire information about British policy more easily in Washington, or in the
corridors of NATO headquarters or at Strasbourg than they can
in Westminster.'[1] Are politicians to be enmeshed into silence
because they are given information widely known abroad?
Facts that are not generally known have a compulsive aura.
David Riesman in his analysis of attitudes to public affairs has
named one category the 'inside dopester',[2] being a person more
concerned to know what *is* going on than to decide what
should go on. If secret committees attract people who like sitting
in secret committees, they will be of little help in guiding action.
And although information is important it must not dominate
judgement to the exclusion of all else. It can be wrong. It can
quickly become out of date. It can divert attention from the
need for other sorts of information. Above all, it can seduce
decision-makers into ignoring principle.

Another obstacle to a confidential committee lies in the
appointment of its members. If they were to be given access to
the innermost official secrets, presumably they would need to be,
or become, privy councillors so as to be bound by oath. If some
lesser degree of access were given, then its members might be

[1] 'Public Opinion and Foreign Policy' in *International Affairs*, (1964),
Vol. 40, p. 33.
[2] *The Lonely Crowd* (O.U.P., 1950).

taken on trust, especially since a much higher standard of confidentiality exists in select committees than in unofficial party gatherings. Yet the concept of 'trustworthy' in this connexion is open to differing interpretations. Would there develop a system of undercover vetting designed to keep off the committee any Members whose reliability had been questioned—albeit for no good reason? Any such prospect is highly unpleasant. Overall, the balance of advantage is against foreign policy discussion *in camera*.

By elimination there remains the possibility of an investigating committee not shrouded by absolute secrecy. This could take one of two main forms, an orthodox Select Committee or a public arena type of arrangement with the Press and even television cameras present, as has been developed in the United States' Congress. The advantage of open confrontation between Ministers or civil servants on one side and backbench Members on the other—as with the pattern of the US Senate Foreign Relations Committee—is that public discussion of major issues would be greatly stimulated. Had a Commons' committee held televised hearings on the Common Market issue in 1962, the educational effect would have been substantial: the court-room element in an investigatory process introduces a sense of drama absent from other forms of discussion and would help to attract a wide audience. Would not such a jamboree be politically unacceptable? It would foul the principle that Ministers are responsible to the Commons as a whole and not to any section of the House. The concept of civil service anonymity would be shattered. Before an investigating committee Ministers would lose much of the advantage they now enjoy at question-time, for their examination would be impromptu and not limited to two minutes on one topic. Were a Minister to defend his policies convincingly under conditions of vast publicity, the political gain to the Government would be great: were he to fail, the damage would be substantial. Would Ministers be willing to take this gamble? What strains would such proceedings impose on party discipline? Certainly, televised committee hearings do not fit easily into the traditions of the British Parliament and are not yet within the realm of probability.

A traditional Select Committee would be open to fewer objections. With the development of the work of the Estimates

Committee and the Nationalized Industries Committee, civil servants have become used to coming to Westminster to explain Departmental policies. Their anonymity may be dented but no one feels that their political impartiality is impaired. Of course, the parallel is not exact. The boundary between policy and administration is ill-defined but the emphasis of the Estimates and Nationalized Industries Committees is decidedly on administration: any effective Foreign Affairs Committee would have to concentrate on policy. Thus it would be a more radical innovation than the type of specialized body advocated by the Study of Parliament Group, and the Group was wise to recommend that a start be made with committees on domestic topics where the problems of secrecy are not acute. If the new machinery of investigation were applied first to less troubled areas of state activity, it would commence under the most favourable conditions and, if judged successful, might then be extended to foreign affairs. David Coombes has argued that specialized committees would make a greater contribution to the critical and educational role of the Commons if they could generally avoid voting and work on the non-party pattern of the financial committees and the Nationalized Industries Committee.[1] No doubt this is true. Yet in the case of foreign affairs one must accept that there is little possibility of Members working on a consensual basis. Their deliberations could still illuminate Government policies and reactions even should a propensity to vote attract attention from party whips. And because of the tension within the Labour Party on foreign policy, it is not certain that votes in the committee would always follow lines of party allegiance.

Any new committee structure of this nature would require new thinking about the relationships between Ministers and the committees of the House. Yet these relationships are already in a process of change: the second reading of some Bills can now go to a committee. And if a committee can question a Minister—in what sense does the Minister become responsible to the committee? He becomes answerable to it. He might even be censured by it should the committee make an unfavourable report to the House, but in normal circumstances this is unlikely since the

[1] *The Member of Parliament and the Administration* (Allen & Unwin, 1966), Ch. 1.

committee will have a majority of government supporters. The central fact is that no Minister can ever be responsible to a group of Members in the sense of being dismissable by it—this ultimate sanction must remain with the whole House and will always be restrained by the claims of party loyalty. Nevertheless, a Foreign Affairs Committee could make life more awkward for a Foreign Secretary and damage his reputation: alternatively he might convince the Committee of the wisdom of his policies and use it to blunt parliamentary criticism. Either consequence is possible. The real question is whether this reform is likely to serve a valuable function in increasing public and parliamentary understanding of international issues and would help to break down the barrier between the experience of Westminster and that of Whitehall.

A Select Committee would make periodic reports to the House; these, combined with a record of evidence received by the Committee, would add to the information available to Members. Yet how far could Ministers or civil servants explain policy adequately if their evidence were to be published? Much of foreign policy is based on an assessment of the motives and probable future actions of foreign governments. To speculate publicly about these matters is virtually impossible for anyone in a responsible position: on the other hand, this is not the type of material that requires the protection of the privy councillors' oath. Foreign affairs are not as secret as defence policy. Diplomatic Correspondents in Fleet Street get much fuller briefings from Whitehall than do Military Correspondents. Ministers may not mind their assessment of a situation being known, provided that they are not committed publicly in conditions that invite open challenge. Perhaps a Foreign Affairs Committee would be gravely hampered unless provision were made that some of its evidence could be unpublished. To avoid the establishment of any distinction between an inner group on the Committee and other Members, unpublished evidence could be made available for Members in the Library on the strict understanding it must not be quoted. Admittedly this is a compromise formula designed to meet the objections to secrecy and the need for it. The compromise might not work well but it is worth a trial. All the alternatives suffer overwhelming objections.

To return from speculation about the future to current reality, there have been moves which seem to bring specialist committees a little nearer. In December, 1965, the Estimates Committee reshaped the pattern of its sub-committees so that each of them has responsibility for a specific sector of State activity. One sub-committee was nominated to deal with defence and overseas affairs. But the existence of this group of Members is a poor guide to how a committee investigating policy might be expected to work. The Estimates Committee still has restricted terms of reference. Further, the Members of the sub-committee on defence and overseas affairs are not Members who are prominent in public criticism of the Government's foreign policy. However, any investigating body of the type discussed above could be expected to attract some of the leading backbench opponents of the Government. And if such a body is nearer, it has certainly not come over the horizon. The Prime Minister in the 1966 debate on the Queen's Speech ventilated the possibility of establishing committees to enquire into the administration of some home departments—but indicated that he was not convinced that there should be parallel committees dealing with foreign policy and defence.[1]

[1] H.C. Deb., Vol. 727, cols. 76–7. See also p. 175 *infra.*

CHAPTER IX

The Influence of Parliament

THE ROLE OF OPPOSITION

THE initiative in foreign policy decisions comes normally from the Prime Minister or Foreign Secretary: their proposals are subject, at least in theory, to Cabinet approval. The Prime Minister may choose to create an informal inner Cabinet of Ministers whose advice carries weight with him. Neville Chamberlain had such a group and Eden formed a Suez Committee to prepare action against Nasser. According to Lord Butler, the Cabinet if asked 'would probably not have agreed to set up such a Committee'.[1] But the decision-makers, be they the whole Cabinet or part of it, are subject to many pressures—the attitude of other states, what is thought to be their probable reaction to certain eventualities, the strategic situation (if armed conflict is even a remote possibility), the advice of Foreign Office officials at home and abroad and the views of Parliament. Thus the legislature is but one of many competing influences and is less potent on foreign affairs than on domestic issues largely because any international problem is not wholly under British control.

It is still of importance that Ministers are answerable to Parliament. The challenge of criticism generates argument and forces Ministers to produce justification for their actions. The strength of a challenge and the influence it wields must depend on the nature of its support. This is not merely a question of numbers and of formal voting in the division lobbies: the views of a handful of respected and experienced Members on the Government benches will make a bigger impact on Ministers than the views of a much larger group of Members on the other side of the House. Nevertheless, numbers have some signifi-

[1] Third Programme broadcast, September, 1965.

cance. If leaders of the official Opposition are in broad agreement with the Government, then criticism from other sources is
easily brushed aside. Thus Churchill's warnings in the nineteen-
thirties went largely unheeded and the more recent controversies
over German rearmament and nuclear weapons had no effect on
Government policy. Especially in time of crisis Ministers are
keen to achieve a front-bench consensus if at all possible.
Opposition opinion is also more potent when the Government's majority in the Commons is small. These two factors
taken together help to explain the mild response of the
Wilson Government to Rhodesia's declaration of independence
in 1965.

In foreign affairs the official Opposition is in a curious
situation. It has no responsibility for the nation's policies but, if
it urges the Government to moderate its attitude, then its
criticism may lead foreign opinion to anticipate a weakening of
the British position. Clearly, this could cause damage in any
international negotiations and be thought contrary to the
national interest. Conservatives took this view of Gaitskell's
objections to the Suez adventure and the Conservative attitude
to Rhodesia is another example. Yet if the Opposition think
that Government policy is leading to unjustified war, it cannot
be expected to restrain its complaints. Another difficulty facing
the official Opposition is that if it condemns a treaty or agreement made by Ministers, the question arises immediately of how
the Opposition would act if returned to power. Will it renounce
the pact and default on our international obligations? The
dilemma is one which Opposition leaders try to avoid. Yet
democracy may be incompatible with continuity of foreign
policy.

Opposition policy can have other side-effects. It may influence not only hostile states but also potential allies. According
to Saul Rose, the Labour Party's acquiesence in 1954 to German
rearmament helped to persuade M. Mendès-France and, therefore, the French Government to accept it also.[1] Alternatively
if the two front-benches are in agreement when Ministers are
attacked by their own nominal supporters, then the Opposition
attitude may add to Government difficulties. Ernest Bevin,

---

[1] *Political Studies*, June 1966, Vol. XIV, p. 144.

Foreign Secretary in the Attlee Government, was often accused of carrying on Conservative policies. Earl Avon, then Anthony Eden the Conservative foreign affairs spokesman, wrote of this period: 'In Parliament I usually followed him (Bevin) in debate and I would publicly have agreed with him more if I had not been anxious to embarrass him less'.[1] Thus bi-partisanship in foreign policy can still be accompanied by some parliamentary shadow boxing.

The mood of Parliament can be of crucial importance when bargaining with other states is in progress. Our negotiators may assert that no further concession is possible because it would not be acceptable to parliamentary opinion. This could be a convenient tactic, or it could be true. During the Common Market negotiations Ministers kept a watchful eye on their own supporters in the Commons. Whether the element of uncertainty in the backbenchers' attitude was welcome to Ministers depended on how keen the individual Minister was to join: the hesitations made it more difficult to reach agreement but they improved the likelihood that agreement, if reached, would be relatively favourable. An uncertain parliament can be a serious handicap to a negotiator. In international bargaining concessions are often emphasized in order to induce a *quid pro quo* from the other side. But if a negotiator is already under attack at home, any public stress on concessions made will strengthen the case of the critics.[2]

It is a commonplace that good relations with the public and a good private understanding with Opposition leaders will assist the success of any Government policy. Secrecy may be convenient in diplomatic negotiations; it makes more possible the use of surprise of bluff, it dampens controversy and prevents concessions being publicised as weakness.[3] But secrecy reduces public and parliamentary understanding. It renders Government action less explicable. There develops an element of unreality in the way that Ministers present their case, an unreality that is exposed as more information becomes available. In a democratic community the long-run chances of a leakage of

[1] *Full Circle* (Cassell, 1960), p. 5.
[2] Cf. F. C. Iklé, *How Nations Negotiate* (Harper and Row, 1964), Ch. 8.
[3] For further discussion of these points see R. Dahl, *Congress and Foreign Policy* (Harcourt Brace, 1950), pp. 257–60.

information must be high. Meanwhile there is little that Parliament can do to prevent Ministers being evasive.

Sometimes Opposition leaders are kept in touch with secret developments and sometimes not. Lord Robens, who was 'shadow' Foreign Secretary at the time of Suez, has admitted to utter astonishment at the Cabinet's reaction to the Israeli invasion of Egypt, although he was dining at 10 Downing Street when the news came through. Robens clearly knew nothing of the clandestine negotiations with France and Israel. If the Opposition are surprised in this way their reactions are more likely to be explosive. Throughout the Suez affair there was an utter lack of confidence between Government and Opposition leaders. Much of the Conservative criticism of Gaitskell at this period was based on his change of attitude between August and September, since his vigorous condemnation in August of Nasser's nationalization of the Canal had led to the belief that Labour would support strong action. But Gaitskell's speech in the August debate was founded on a private assurance from Eden that no use of armed force against Egypt was contemplated. Another such assurance was obtained later the same month. When it became clear that military action was being prepared, Gaitskell's tone changed.[1]

A Cabinet may be unwise to undertake precipitate measures in the international sphere when opinion in the country is deeply divided. Grave cleavages of opinion may develop. Organized labour may threaten strike action: in 1920 at the time of the Soviet-Polish conflict London dockers refused to load arms destined for Poland, and strong hints of British intervention to help Poland faded away. The armed forces will also be dissatisfied unless they feel that their sacrifices are demanded by a united national will. Yet there are no constitutional means of checking a Cabinet so long as Ministers retain a majority in the Commons. Even the fading theory of the mandate—that the actions of a Government should be restricted to its election pledges—has never been seriously applied to foreign affairs. It is a conservative doctrine designed to hamper radical domestic reforms and to provide justification for the continuing existence of the House of Lords. But conservative opinion

---

[1] Douglas Jay in *Hugh Gaitskell*, edited by W. T. Rodgers (Thames and Hudson, 1964), pp. 101–3.

would resist any notion that a Government should be inhibited by a constitutional theory from acting as it saw fit in the national interest in its relationships with other states. Left-wing politicians have little sympathy for the mandate doctrine. So few opponents of the Common Market argued that the negotiations were constitutionally improper, although the project of joining had not been put to the electorate either in 1955 or 1959. Probably had Britain entered the Community in 1963 a general election would have been held in that year dominated by the Common Market issue. However, this would have been smart political tactics rather than a constitutional necessity.

Is an economic negotiation necessarily to be treated equally with the issue of starting a war? Certainly it is tempting, if idealistic, to argue that the British Government should not initiate military action without general consent from the other major parties. There are practical and ethical considerations to support such a proposal. General approval is undeniably an aid to a military enterprise. Of even greater weight is the argument that a decision to unleash the horror of modern armaments should not be taken by a simple majority vote. To require virtual unanimity is, however, essentially a 'do nothing' doctrine which must weaken the authority of any state which adopts it. To give the Opposition a permanent veto is to offer power without responsibility: it would also encourage extreme opinion within the Opposition by making dissidents more significant.[1]

In the harsh reality of British politics, granted that the mandate doctrine is discarded, can there be no moral check on Government actions? There is just a little. To take the case of foreign affairs, should a Party win a general election after advocating certain principles of international behaviour and shortly afterwards appear to act contrary to those principles—then the Government would face charges of bad faith both in and out of Parliament. Thus in 1935 the Hoare-Laval pact on the Italian-Abyssinian conflict was a denial of the concept of collective security and support for the League of Nations which Conservatives had advocated at the election held a few weeks before. The subsequent resignation of Sir Samuel Hoare is a

[1] J. M. Buchanan and G. Tullock in *The Calculus of Consent* (University of Michigan Press, 1962) set out a logical case for requiring unanimity as a pre-condition of political action.

162

useful reminder that even in foreign affairs Parliament can and should make a Government uncomfortable if it strays from electoral pledges.

Parliament is utterly impotent if a Government makes secret agreements with other states. Half-a-century ago hidden diplomacy attracted much criticism and was widely condemned especially by Radical opinion. Yet it still occurs: Governments both Labour and Conservative have found it expedient. In 1952 Winston Churchill, then Prime Minister, informed the Commons that in May of the previous year the Labour Government had told the United States 'that in the event of heavy air attacks from bases in China upon United Nations forces in Korea they would associate themselves with action not confined to Korea'.[1] Subsequently former Labour Ministers objected to this revelation but they did not suggest that Churchill's statement was inaccurate. Another secret pact of outstanding importance was the 1943 Quebec Agreement between Churchill and Roosevelt on the use of tube alloys—the code name used for atomic weapons. The agreement, which was made public in 1954,[2] bound Britain and the United States never to use these weapons against each other and never to use them against third parties without mutual consent. It was, in fact, an example of the unanimity principle discussed above. The British veto was surrendered by the Attlee Government in 1948 by another secret agreement in return for economic advantages arising out of the industrial use of atomic power: three years later Prime Minister Attlee told the House that a wartime agreement with the United States on atomic weapons had been modified but he gave no details.[3] Thus major decisions were taken quite unknown to Parliament. The conditions surrounding the Quebec Agreement were quite exceptional. The action of the Labour Government is more questionable; whether Labour Members in the 1945 Parliament would have approved—had they known —is doubtful. Secret agreements are always unsatisfactory in that they always present the problem of whether succeeding Governments will feel themselves bound by the word of their predecessors. In the nature of things they cannot be under public or legislative pressure to honour an agreement they dislike.

[1] H.C. Deb., Vol. 496, col. 969.   [2] 1953–54, Cmd. 9123, xxxiii.
[3] H.C. Deb., Vol. 483, cols. 715–6.

THE EXTENT OF INFLUENCE

Certainly the record of Parliament on foreign affairs is unimpressive. In the volume on foreign policy in the official history of the Second World War,[1] Parliament is mentioned merely as a place where Ministers made speeches or statements. Debates, in war or peace, tend to be bitty and inconclusive. Ministerial speeches should be phrased with extreme care because of potential reaction abroad. Damaging misunderstandings must be avoided. Critical backbench speeches tend to be predictable: one reason why Churchill's parliamentary reputation suffered in the nineteen-thirties was that his constant reassertion of the German danger became a bore. A lesser-known Member with something original to say may not be called on to speak. Foreign affairs are not thought of as a fruitful field for parliamentary endeavour. Younger and more able Members, the potential Ministers, will take an interest in foreign policy but will rarely specialize in it. Many come to Parliament with no experience of international politics and constituency pressures impel them to spend much time on domestic problems. Although an immediate issue concentrates debate and crystallizes opinion, the quality of attention is still disappointing. In his detailed study of the Manchurian crisis 1931–3, Bassett argued that parliamentary debates of the period failed to provide an adequate picture of public opinion.[2] Another example was the reaction to military intervention by the United States in the Dominican Republic in 1965. This expedition was undoubtedly contrary to the United Nations Charter (Article 24), but Britain supported the United States in the Security Council in spite of the declared intention of the Labour Government to do what it could to strengthen the United Nations. However, the Commons paid little attention to Dominica partly because much of its time was being consumed by the committee stage of the Budget and also because Left-wing Members were more concerned about Vietnam. Perhaps British opinion was not deeply concerned with either Manchuria or Dominica—but the

[1] Sir Llewellyn Woodward, *British Foreign Policy in the Second World War* (H.M.S.O., 1962).
[2] R. Bassett, *Democracy and Foreign Policy* (London School of Economics, 1952), p. xviii.

Commons should educate the public mood, not merely reflect it. On long-term issues, Parliament is even less stimulating. Many Members are cautious about making statements on topics where party policy is undecided and the progression of events is highly uncertain. Speculation about the future provides hostages to fortune. The idea that the Commons acts as a public Grand Inquest of the Nation is but a partially realised ideal in relation to foreign affairs. Now the mass media increasingly replace it.

Private discussion, of course, is more virile than public discussion—but does nothing to instruct a wider audience. A *Hansard* of the meetings of the Parliamentary Labour Party would be of great interest, but might castrate the arguments. As it is, unofficial reports of meetings appear in the 'serious' newspapers in spite of severe party disapproval. All this is a modern counterpart to the unofficial reporting of Parliamentary debates in the eighteenth century and the attempts to suppress it. On June 15, 1966, the Prime Minister made a major speech to the Parliamentary Labour Party on his East of Suez policy; the meeting approved the policy by 225 votes to 54 and agreed that the text of Wilson's statement be published. This innovation is profoundly unsatisfactory. If the speech were of such great importance—why was it not made in the Commons' Chamber? The consequence of publishing alone the speech of a Party Leader is to give but a partial and misleading impression of Party opinion since the case of those who oppose his view does not get equal publicity. Churchill's wish to have broadcast his wartime speeches to the Commons was not granted for precisely this reason. Wilson's manoeuvre aroused criticism in Labour Party circles and so far has not been repeated. Any device to give the Prime Minister preferential treatment must do great damage to the status of Parliament by overtly transforming it from an arena for debate into a means of manipulating opinion.

What is the effect of public and private parliamentary discussion on foreign policy? If Parliament is in recess when major developments occur and is not recalled, as with Abadan, it must be impotent. Rarely can it be said with certainty that the course of affairs has been changed by an initiative of the legislature. One example is the case of the 1924 treaty with the Soviet

Union.[1] When negotiations between the Foreign Office and the Russian delegation reached the point of breakdown, a group of Labour Members led by E. D. Morel intervened and helped to produce a compromise formula acceptable to both sides. But this endeavour was not successful because the downfall of the Labour Government was speeded by the allegation that the nation's diplomacy was being dominated by extremist back-benchers. How ludicrous was this claim can be seen by a comparison of the disputed draft[2] with the final form of the treaty.[3] Due to the defeat of the Government in the 1924 Election the treaty never came into operation. However, this is still a remarkable case of backbench intervention in the detail of diplomacy. That it occured was due to a unique combination of factors. The Labour Cabinet was inexperienced: it did not appreciate that to seem to allow backbenchers to take over the business of international negotiation would be seized on as a mark of weakness. Many Government supporters in the Commons had been influenced by the campaign of the Union of Democratic Control for democratic foreign policy. The Prime Minister, Ramsay MacDonald, was also Foreign Secretary, leaving the detailed work of the Foreign Office to the Under Secretary, Arthur Ponsonby. Morel, the leader of the backbench negotiators, was exceptionally well-informed on foreign affairs and had been, together with Ponsonby, a dominant figure in the Union of Democratic Control. In these circumstances the gulf that usually divides Ministers from backbenchers disappeared.

Other examples of parliamentary influence if less clear-cut are perhaps of greater significance. A speech by Austen Chamberlain to the Conservative Foreign Affairs Committee is said to have played a large part in the resignation of the Foreign Secretary, Sir Samuel Hoare, in 1935.[4] The mood of the Commons in 1939 may well have strengthened the will of Neville Chamberlain's Government to resist Hitler after the invasion of Poland.

How much effect parliamentary opinion had on the unfolding of the Suez disaster is a matter of controversy which cannot be

[1] R. W. Lyman, *The First Labour Government* (Chapman and Hall, 1957), Ch. IX describes this incident fully.
[2] 1924 Cmd. 2253 xxvi.   [3] 1924 Cmd. 2260 xxvi.
[4] L. S. Amery, *My Political Life* (Hutchinson, 1955), Vol. III, p. 184 *et seq.*

finally settled until some Conservative lips are unsealed and documents become available. But it is certain that a group of Members opposed to the use of force in Egypt met together and let Ministers know that they would be unable to support the policy in the division lobbies. Estimates of the size of this group vary, the highest being about forty. Since only eight abstained in the vote on November 8th, the figure of forty may be thought too high. Yet by this time the Eden Cabinet had accepted the United Nations' call for a cease-fire and fighting had ceased. It followed that by then public abstention could not affect policy—it merely satisfied a Member's conscience at the cost of great trouble with his local constituency organisation. Many potential rebels may have felt it unnecessary to make an unpopular protest when they had, in effect, already got their own way. Whatever the precise number of anti-Suez rebels, they had no leader of national stature and, as their protest was almost wholly conducted in private, it had little impact on public opinion. How far they influenced the vital Cabinet discussion that led to the cease-fire decision is an insoluble problem. It seems that the Cabinet were mainly alarmed by the overseas threat to the stability of sterling, an issue which developed unexpectedly. Had this pressure been lacking, backbench opinion might have gained more attention. Herman Finer has given a detailed account of a 'phone call by Eden to M. Mollet the French Premier consisting of a catalogue of reasons why the British Government had agreed that military action must cease. 'I can't even rely on unanimity among the Conservatives' Eden is supposed to have said.[1] Another item in the catalogue was the attitude of Dr Fisher, Archbishop of Canterbury, whose critical speech in the Lords had received widespread attention.[2]

Perhaps parliamentary opinion had its greatest impact at an earlier stage of the crisis. It was noted above how Gaitskell's attitude changed between August and September when it became clear that the Government were preparing a military expedition. By September the political pressures against the use of force were mounting—internationally because of the work of Dulles, American Secretary of State, in forming the Suez Canal Users' Association, and at home because of the hostility of Labour and

[1] *Dulles over Suez* (Heinemann, 1964), p. 429.
[2] H.L. Deb., Vol. 199, cols. 1293-7.

Liberal opinion. Could this have pushed Eden into accepting the strategem of the Israeli invasion so that he could pretend to be stopping a war, or at least be protecting the Canal, instead of nakedly invading another country? Backbench attitudes, this time of Right-wing Conservatives, also had an effect on the end of the Suez episode. It seems certain that the 1957 decision that British ships should again use the Canal would have been made earlier but for much high Tory resistance.

Parliamentary doubts in 1962 about the Common Market may well have damaged our chances of admission. It is arguable that if the British Government firmly intended to join, then they should have signed the Treaty of Rome first and settled the details afterwards. The French veto would have been avoided by this tactic. However, there were overwhelming obstacles to any dramatic step; it would have weakened our bargaining position and parliamentary opinion was quite unprepared for such an upheaval.[1]

How likely Members are to succeed when urging the Government to act in a particular way must depend on the size of the gap between their views and those of Ministers. At any one time the Government may be exposed to conflicting influences from those advocating a more vigorous pursuit of an existing policy and those wishing for a complete change of direction. Members satisfied with government actions tend to be inert unless they fear that policy may change in a way they strongly dislike. There are three categories of political pressure which may be set out as follows:[2]

Positive pressure=urging firmer action to secure existing ends.

Negative pressure=urging continuation of the *status quo*.

Counter pressure=urging a basic change of policy.

To classify some examples described above: in 1939 the Com-

---

[1] K. Younger, 'Public Opinion and Foreign Policy' in *International Affairs* (1964), pp. 29–31.

[2] There is a logical difficulty about this scheme. If the Government were to have no policy on a problem, i.e. it has no declared ends in view, then any proposals for action, even conflicting proposals, must all be termed counter pressure. But such is the world-wide nature of British interests, the Government will always have a view—most probably that the *status quo* should be preserved—about any problem important enough to come before Parliament.

mons exerted positive pressure to resist German aggression and in 1962 the overall doubt and hesitation about the Common Market amounted to negative pressure. The Suez case is more complex because the same people applied different types of pressure as the action developed. Before force was used against Egypt, Left-wing Conservatives exercised negative pressure, and thereafter counter pressure. Right-wing Tories put on positive pressure throughout this period, but in 1957 when the crisis was over and the issue was the normalization of relations with Egypt and the use of the Canal, this wing of the Party exercised negative pressure. Usually Government backbenchers incline to positive pressure. They will share the same ideals as Ministers but will be more impatient or less aware of immediate practical difficulties. Opposition backbenchers may sometimes want a complete reversal of policy, for example, Right-wing Tories who object to sanctions against Rhodesia, but such is the unity of view on foreign policy that counter pressure is often largely absent. A few Members in 1914 and 1939 opposed the declaration of war (negative pressure) but none urged that we go to war on the side of Germany. Similarly, in relation to the current East-West conflict, the Communist Party has not been represented in the Commons since 1950 although a few Members have had 'neutralist' tendencies.

Pressures from Members may be supported or hampered by other aspects of the international scene. How far this is so in any particular case must be a matter of sophisticated guesswork. Members who seek defence economies and a reduction in our commitments east of Suez may appear to be strengthened by the nation's financial difficulties and the weakness of sterling. But if United States' support for sterling stems from sympathetic appreciation of our presence in Asia—then a reduction in that presence could weaken sterling, at least in the short run. This type of calculation can lead to the view that foreign policy, or any policy, is a mechanical consequence of the balance of pressure on a Cabinet. The degree of unity in a Cabinet, the ideas of Ministers and the nature of their motivation are all of great significance. The Prime Minister is usually deeply involved in foreign affairs and his personal judgement can dominate policy. Obvious examples are Chamberlain's negotiations with Hitler, Macmillan's 'wind of change' speech in South Africa and

Churchill's desire for a summit meeting with the leaders of the Soviet Union after the death of Stalin. In the last case there was no pressure from the Cabinet or the Conservative Party to pursue the idea and absolutely no international encouragement.

Of the three types of persuasion described above, counter pressure is the form least likely to succeed. If it comes from Members on the Government benches, as over Suez, the political consequences may be explosive. Negative pressures are those with the best chance of success, and these may even be welcomed by a Cabinet reluctant to take decisions involving stronger action. It is comforting that in time of peace negative pressures are necessarily of peaceful intent.

THE FUTURE

A very real love for Parliament is at present an important feature of British politics. It is perhaps both an aspect and a buttress of British insularity and conservatism. Yet Parliament is also the corner-stone of our democracy, which the last war was fought to defend, and the centre of a political system which all the main parties accept without question. Even the serious critics of Parliament assail it in sorrow, not in anger; their charge is not that the Commons is an effete or futile institution, but that its procedure should be modernized to increase its effectiveness.

Two suggestions for parliamentary reform have been in vogue. One, for specialized committees, was discussed in the previous Chapter. The other, also come to fruition, is the institution of a Parliamentary Commissioner for Administration to deal with complaints from the public on the model of the Scandinavian Ombudsman: this development, however, will have almost no application to foreign issues. The Commissioner is to be concerned with matters of administration, not policy. Although his remit covers the Foreign Office, it excludes our High Commissions, Embassies, Consular Offices or other Government outposts abroad. To be considered a complaint must be forwarded to the Commissioner by a Member and arise from the rights and obligations in this country of a person who is lawfully present here.[1] So the impact of the Commissioner on

[1] *The Parliamentary Commissioner for Administration*, 1964–65, Cmnd. 2767, para. 6.

the Foreign Office is likely to be minimal. One of the major investigations of the Danish Ombudsman concerned the allegedly lax attitude of the Danish Foreign Ministry towards a diplomat, Ejnar Blechingberg, who was accused of spying and sentenced to eight years imprisonment on charges of espionage.[1] Burgess and Maclean would provide a parallel British case, but it seems unlikely that the British Commissioner will be concerned with matters of security.

It is inevitable that the authority of the British Government—and, therefore, of Parliament—will be reduced by the decline in British status in the world and by weakness of the £ sterling. Today the dominant powers are the United States and the Soviet Union, a fact which governs the world-wide pattern of alliances and pressures. Britain has now slipped down to a secondary position. The grouping of states into blocs is not new, but the present Communist and anti-Communist coalitions are larger in size and less flexible in composition than earlier groups. In spite of the French example, it is difficult for a second-rank nation to exercise independent initiative on major world problems. The new multi-racial Commonwealth which has replaced the Empire is clearly no longer an organization that will provide automatic support for British policies. As the nation-state declines (or as the second-rank nation-states decline), international organizations achieve greater significance. This can be illustrated simply by two outstanding examples. The United Nations has had a major effect on British policy in Suez and Cyprus. Membership of the European Economic Community would impose major restraints on Britain with regard to its domestic policies and would thus limit further the freedom of action of Cabinet and Parliament. One should not regret a tendency for Parliament to become enmeshed in an international web if this will serve to reduce the dangers of war or promote prosperity by breaking down artificial barriers to trade.

The question of British entry into the Community raises two quite separate issues about the status of Parliament. The first problem is how Parliament should control the way in which the British vote is cast in the Council of Ministers of the Community. Should we be satisfied with the usual convention that

[1] David Williams, *Not in the Public Interest* (Hutchinson, 1965), pp. 212–3.

Ministers are *post facto* answerable to Parliament and dismissable in the highly unlikely event of an adverse vote or a Cabinet split? Or should the spirit of the Ponsonby rule be invoked so that regulations coming before the Council of Ministers should first be presented to the British Parliament for its opinion? In this way Parliament could formalize its control over how the British vote were cast—even if it could not control the final decision of the Community. The German law approving the Treaty of Rome has provisions to this effect.[1]

The other issue that arises is the possibility of a conflict of laws between regulations made under the Rome Treaty and the existing domestic law of this country. Before entering the Common Market the Government would have a moral duty to ensure that the British Parliament was prepared to accept whatever changes in our law might be needed to harmonize it with our new international obligations. If Parliament is ready, on certain terms, to agree to enter the Common Market, then it must accept the whole of the consequences. The difficulty is that Parliament (at the initiative of the Cabinet) may subsequently want to change a law so as to make it inconsistent with the rules of the Economic Community. In Britain the sovereignty of Parliament is a basic constitutional doctrine; this implies, in the classic formulation, that Parliament may give orders to all and receive orders from none. A logical corollary of this doctrine is that no Parliament can bind its successors.[2] In terms of British law there can be no means of preventing a future Parliament from breaking the rules of the Community if it should so choose. The consequence must be a clash between British law and international law. Exactly the same position would arise in an aggravated form if Britain, once having entered the Common Market, decided to leave it. Such an eventuality would create a major crisis in international politics; there would be heavy pressures on the British Government and Parliament to avoid it.

A decision to enter the Common Market would affect many branches of British law.[3] The dominant purpose of the Treaty

---

[1] P. B. Keenan, 'Some Legal Consequences of Britain's Entry into the European Common Market', in *Public Law* 1962, pp. 332–3.

[2] *Ellen Street Estates Ltd. v. Ministry of Health* (1934), 1 K.B. 590.

[3] See Keenan, pp. 335–42.

of Rome is to secure free and fair competition between producers in its area. Member states are not to impose lower charges on their own products than on those of other member states. This principle must alter the pattern of indirect taxation. The Rome Treaty also prohibits restrictive practices if these are likely to affect trade between member-states: British law on monopolies and restrictive practices would have to be changed. Provisions governing the free movement of labour within the community would involve amendment to the Aliens Restriction Acts. Criminal law might also have to be changed in relation to business matters. The law on social insurance, conditions of employment and trade unions would also require to be reviewed to ensure conformity with the Treaty of Rome. Details of the changes required are highly complex and cannot be fully worked out in advance since the framework of the Common Market itself is still evolving. So far there is little public understanding in Britain of the implications of entering Europe. But if Britain were to join, and if the Common Market develops its authority, then the ambit of the British Parliament would shrink. British opinion ought then to pay much greater heed to the working of Common Market institutions and to the economic problems of its European partners. Less attention for the British Parliament would cause its status to fade.

Should this occur, would other international assemblies, notably the Consultative Assembly of the Council of Europe, benefit from the diminution of Parliament? Probably not. Advisory bodies are essentially unexciting. No deliberative body operates to its own satisfaction, or enjoys much public esteem, unless it has precise tasks to perform which are carried out by an executive free from external control. These conditions are not fulfilled by the institutions of the Common Market where the vital decisions are taken by the Council of Ministers who meet together as representatives of member-governments. At present, members of the Consultative Assembly provide little more than a channel of communication between the Assembly and public opinion in the member-states. Since international bodies meet but occasionally and attract little attention, the channel is very narrow and works intermittently. The conclusion must be that, unless the Treaty of Rome develops into a single federal state, the influence of the national

173

legislatures in the Community will decline without any compensating growth of an international legislature. This involves a weakening of democratic tendencies within the system.

Even if the nation shies away from integration with Europe, the outlook for Parliament is less than rosy. There is now general appreciation of how much it suffers from the concentration of power in the Cabinet and even further in the hands of the Prime Minister. The shift in the balance of power between legislature and executive dates back into the last century and coincided with the increase in party discipline. It has been shown above that the tendency for the Prime Minister to play a dominant role in foreign affairs is not new; certainly in this sphere the fashionable theory that sees Britain as moving towards a system of 'Presidential' government is itself a little behind the times. But in any case, the development of Presidential government affects the relationship between the Prime Minister and his Cabinet rather than the influence of Parliament.

The much more serious threat to Parliament is the competition of the mass media, especially television. Sir Charles Webster has written that in the post-war period the authority of Parliament has declined because its debates are less fully reported and the public goes to other sources of information and instruction.[1] There is plenty of recent evidence to support this view. The greatest public success achieved by Michael Stewart during his period as Foreign Secretary was his televised speech to the Oxford teach-in on Vietnam: this performance earned a comment from *The Observer*[2] that 'Mr Stewart himself emerged for the first time as a Foreign Secretary of exceptional calibre'. Ministerial pronouncements on foreign affairs are increasingly made, not to the Commons, but to television cameras; Parliament may be in recess at a critical moment or the airport news conference may simply provide a publicity opportunity too good to be missed.

I conclude by reference to Bagehot's classic statement of the functions of Parliament. Three of the five functions have particular application to foreign affairs. To use his terminology, these are the expressive, teaching and informing functions. The first of these tasks, 'to express the mind of the English people' is

[1] *The Art and Practice of Diplomacy* (Chatto and Windus, 1961), p. 53.
[2] June 20, 1965.

performed moderately well, if only because public opinion is normally inert on international questions. The teaching and informing functions overlap. Here Parliament has grave shortcomings. How far the Commons are able to teach and inform must depend on the resources available to Members, their own abilities and the way in which parliamentary business is organized.

The biggest single aid towards improving the information available to Members would be to break down the invisible barrier that divides Westminster from Whitehall and to establish the practice that Members talk freely to the Civil Service. Civil servants do already talk about their business to friends with varying degrees of discretion: this does not destroy the hallowed traditions of the anonymity and impartiality of public officials, nor does it arouse the Official Secrets Acts. But if ever civil servants talk to Members they are ultra-cautious. One recently elected Labour Member told me that it had become much more difficult for him to get material from official quarters since his election.[1] Civil servants possess precisely the sort of information which would be of most value to Members, i.e. what sort of considerations are uppermost in the minds of Ministers and Departments at the stage when decisions have to be made. Obviously Ministers will resist the idea that such knowledge might be passed on regularly to their political opponents. Combined with the special degree of secrecy that enshrouds the Foreign Office, Ministerial attitudes make easy congress between British diplomats and Members seem highly unlikely for the foreseeable future.

In terms of academic qualifications the House of Commons elected in 1966 is better equipped than any of its predecessors; in consequence, backbench frustration at the traditional practices of Parliament has reached a new peak. The Leader of the House, R. H. S. Crossman, reflected the mood by admitting that the balance between executive and legislature has swung too far in favour of the executive. As an experiment, two specialized committees have been established, one for science and technology, the other for agriculture. The Commons will also meet on Monday and Wednesday mornings to deal with non-contentious

[1] This comment referred particularly to the Scottish Office.

175

business, partly in order to reduce the number of late-night sittings. These changes are a move in the right direction but are too limited to endow the Commons with much added authority. Yet it is authority—as opposed to power—that the Commons must conserve as a pre-condition of an effective educational role. A teacher who is not respected is not heeded. On no topic is public education more vital than foreign affairs, both because of the importance of the issues and the high level of general unconcern. Meanwhile if Ministers increasingly address the public other than through Parliament, the stature of Parliament will be diminished. The British legislature will have to force itself to meet the challenge of mass media if it is to teach and inform the public and if it is to have any real influence over the direction of public policy.

Three conclusions are inescapable. Parliament must allow greater flexibility in its timetable and permit greater backbench initiative, particularly through freer use of Standing Order 9.[1] A Foreign Affairs Committee must be established—at least as an experiment. Finally, television cameras must be admitted to the Commons' Chamber.

[1] While this book was in the press, the Select Committee on Procedure recommended a modification to the wording of this Standing Order designed to give the Speaker more discretion in permitting its use. *Inter alia* the lack of direct ministerial responsibility for the subject raised would no longer be a complete barrier to its discussion under the Standing Order; instead the Speaker would 'have regard to the extent of the responsibility of Ministers of the Crown'. The Procedure Committee also suggested that the ballot for the right to move private members' motions be held weekly instead of fortnightly to increase topicality. 1966–7 (282).

APPENDIX. TIME DEVOTED BY THE COMMONS TO FOREIGN AFFAIRS

FOREIGN AFFAIRS: ANALYSIS BY PROCEDURE

Procedure	*1947–1948* Days	Hrs. Mins.	*1952–1953* Days	Hrs. Mins.	*1957–1958* Days	Hrs. Mins.	*1962–1963* Days	Hrs. Mins.	*Total* Days	Hrs. Mins.
Debate on the Address	3	5·51	1	4·54	1	4·45	3	9·06	8	24·36
Adjournment Motion										
Daily	5	30·06	9	46·09	4	25·25	3	15·13	21	116·53
Holiday	10	5·31	5	4·01	2	0·53	3	1·22	20	11·47
on a Supply Day	3	3·09					2	2·12	5	5·21
	1	6·20							1	6·20
Government Motion							4	26·17	4	26·17
Opposition Motion							1	3·41	1	3·41
Private Member's Motion			1	0·25	1	4·54			2	5·19
Private Member's Bill							1	0·40	1	0·40
Ten Minute Rule Bill							1	0·12	1	0·12
Government Bill	3	19·37	2	2·00			2	2·16	7	23·53
Consolidated Fund Bill	2	2·09	1	3·05	1	0·21	2	5·47	6	11·22
Committee of Supply	2	6·57	3	10·36	2	12·28			7	30·01
Approval of a Statutory Instrument			1	0·12	1	0·11	2	2·18	4	2·41
Rejection of a Statutory Instrument			1	1·49					1	1·49
Ministerial Statement	8	1·54	13	3·23	4	0·52	11	3·34	36	9·43
Personal Statement							1	0·02	1	0·02
Questions (See below)		18·43		19·49		15·03		14·02		67·37
TOTALS		100·17		96·23		64·52		86·42		348·14

FOREIGN AFFAIRS: ANALYSIS OF QUESTIONS

Type of Question	1947–1948		1952–1953		1957–1958		1962–1963		Total	
	No.	Hrs. Mins.	No.	Hrs. Mins.	No.	Hrs. Mins.	No.	Hrs. Mins.	No.	Hrs. Mins.
Foreign Office Questions	711	17·13	557	12·22	410	10·42	184	8·25	1862	48·42
Private Notice Questions	16	1·10	14	1·42	2	0·10	6	0·32	38	3·34
Questions answered at end of question-time	2	0·14	11	1·27	2	0·21	8	0·22	23	2·24
Prime Minister's Questions	5	0·06	122	4·18	132	3·50	97	4·43	356	12·57
Written answers	402	—	242	—	280	—	439	—	1363	—
TOTALS	1136	18·43	946	19·49	826	15·03	734	14·02	3642	67·37

INDEX

Abyssinia, 162
Aden, 51, 112
adjournment motions, 74, 83, 91, 92, 101, 102, 103, 108, 177
uses of, 88–90
Agadir crisis, 23
Aliens Restriction Acts, 173
Allaun, F. *M.P.*, 110, 137n., 139n., 141
Allighan, G. *M.P.*, 135n.
Almond, G. A., 33n.
Amalgamated Engineering Union, 125
Amery, L. S. *M.P.*, 166n.
Amnesty International, 128
Angell, N. *M.P.*, 25
Anglo-French Convention 1904, 23, 43, 50
Anglo-German Convention 1898, 50
Anglo-Rhodesian Society, 128
Anti-Common Market League, 129–30
aristocracy, role in foreign affairs, 13, 19, 20, 28–9, 70
Asia, defence commitments in, 124, 134, 142, 165, 169
Astor, 3rd Viscount, 114
Astor, J. J. *M.P.*, 120
atomic research, communication of information, 63n.
Attlee, C. R. *M.P.*, 1st Earl, 63n., 97, 124, 142, 151, 160, 163
Avon, 1st Earl of *see* Eden, Sir R. Anthony

backbenchers:
amendments to Queen's Speech by, 140–1
bills, 80, 94, 102, 103, 112–13
interests, 77, 110
international activities of, 138
lack of information for, 63–6

lobbying of Ministers by, 141
motions by, 20–1, 67, 90, 94–5, 138–40, 176, 177
1924 treaty with Russia and, 165–6
participation in debates, 76, 77–8, 89, 90, 114
party research facilities and, 57, 58
questions and, 87, 88, 110
Radicals concerned to strengthen, 20–2
time, 46, 67, 81, 90, 94–5
Bagehot, W., 20, 22–3, 46, 174–5
Baldwin, S. *M.P.*, 1st Earl, 46, 70
Balfour, A. J. *M.P.*, 27, 83, 87
Barker, A., 75n.
Bartholomew, D. J., 140n.
Bassett, R., 124n., 164
Belgium, 40 *see also* Benelux countries
Bell, G. K. A. *bp.*, 98
Beloff, M., 152
Benelux countries, 53n., 80
Berkeley, H. J. *M.P.*, 94, 108
Berlin Conference 1954, 142
Berrington, H. B., 140n.
Bevan, A. *M.P.*, 75, 131, 137
Bevin, E. *M.P.*, 135, 159–60
Biggs-Davison, J. A. *M.P.*, 108, 110, 112
bills, on foreign affairs, 112 *see also* backbenchers, bills
Birch, A. H., 125n.
Bishop, D. G., 14, 39n.
bishops, foreign affairs debates and, 98, 99n., 167
Blechingberg, E., 171
blue books *see* parliamentary papers
Boer War, 30
Boothby, R. J. G. *M.P.*, Baron, 120

179

Index

Index

Index

Shinwell, E. *M.P.*, 92n., 110, 140
Sidgwick, H., 22n.
Silverman, S. S. *M.P.*, 139n.
Smith, Ian D., 99n. 122, 127 *see also* Rhodesia
Smithers, P. H. B. O. *M.P.*, 100
Society for Cultural Relations with the U.S.S.R., 128
Somali Republic, 47
South Africa, 30, 103, 108, 169
South Africa Act 1962, 80
Soviet Union, 30, 41, 51n., 54, 55, 83, 97, 104, 106, 111, 142, 161, 170
  as major power, 14, 28, 38, 171
  diplomatic recognition of, 46–7
  1924 treaty with, 165–6
  secret treaties published by, 27
Spain, 30, 46–7, 52, 54, 102, 124, 132
Speaker, 106, 140
  adjournment motions and, 89, 90, 176n.
  debates and, 77
  Library controlled by, 62n.
  Ministerial statements and, 91
  questions and, 83, 85, 91
Spearman, Sir Alexander C. M. *M.P.*, 107
Spectator, 56n., 121
Spitz, D., 31n.
Stalin, I. V., 170
Standing Joint Committee on Indian Affairs, 150
Stanhope, 7th Earl, 98–9
Statutory Instruments, 81–2, 102, 103, 113, 115, 177
Stewart, J. D., 118n.
Stewart, R. M. M. *M.P.*, 51, 126, 135, 136, 174
Stonehouse, J. T. *M.P.*, 110
Strang, W., 1st Baron, 71, 88n.
Study of Parliament Group, 147, 155
Sudan Agreement, 44
Suez Canal Users' Association, 167
Suez Committee, 158

Suez crisis, 39, 75, 129, 134, 139, 159, 171
  Church criticism of, 98, 99n., 167
  compensation payments resulting from, 112, 113
  constituencies and, 122, 127
  Ministers refuse information on, 65, 161
  Parliamentary opinion and, 40, 166–8, 169
  party discipline and, 120–1, 141, 167, 170
  secret diplomacy and, 34, 161
Suez Group, 134
Supply, Committee of, 67, 74–5, 95, 177
Sutherland, 15th or 16th Earl of, 82
Swanwick, H. M., 24n.
Swingler, S. T. *M.P.*, 110
Swinton, 1st Viscount, 44

Tangier, status of, 29
Taylor, A. J. P., 19n., 50n.
Taylor, S. J. L. *M.P.*, Baron, 97
television, 48, 50, 78, 88, 91, 92, 154, 174, 176
Temperley, H. W. V., 50n.
Ten-Minute Rule Bills, 102, 112, 177
Thomas, P. J. M. *M.P.*, 100, 111
Times, 66n., 137, 152
Tocqueville, A. de, 17–18, 30
Trade, President of Board of, 68
Trade Commission Service, 95
trade unions, 117, 119, 125, 126, 130, 136, 137n.
Trades Union Congress, 124
Transport House, International Department, 58
Travis, M., 79n.
treaties:
  debates on, 20–9, 42–6
  forms of, 41, 45
  invalidated by changes in law, 81, 172
  legislation consequent on, 78–81

189

treaties—*contd.*
Parliamentary assent needed for, 42
Parliamentary control, 20–9, 34, 42–6
publication of, 27, 50–2
ratification of, 41, 42, 43–5, 51, 52
royal prerogative and, 36, 41–6
secret, publication of, 27, 50
U.S. Constitution and, 17, 44
Treaty of Rome, 104, 168, 172–3
see also European Economic Community
Treaty of Trianon, 55
Treaty of Utrecht, 43
Treaty of Versailles, 28, 29, 43
Treaty of Washington, 21
Treaty Series, contents of, 51–2
Trevelyan, C. P. *M.P.*, 25, 40
Trevelyan, G. M., 43n.
Tullock, G., 162n.
Turkey, 27, 30, 44, 83
Turner, A. C., 18n.

U.S.S.R. *see* Soviet Union
unanimity, as requisite for political action, 162, 163
Unesco, 51
Union of Democratic Control, 24–9 *passim*, 34, 43, 166
United Nations, 51, 61, 69, 90, 102, 108, 115, 143, 163, 164
Congo action, 108, 110, 114, 129, 134
Suez crisis and, 129, 167, 171
United Nations Association, 128, 129
United Nations Parliamentary Group, 133
United States, 55, 61, 110, 112, 137, 139, 141, 163, 164, 169
as major power, 14, 28, 38, 171
Constitution and foreign relations, 17, 44, 47
declaration of war in, 17, 30n., 38
First World War and, 27–8, 29

Vietnam and, 35, 88, 89, 124, 136, 138, 140, 141, 142
see also Foreign Relations Committee; Library of Congress; MacMahon Act
Universal Postal Convention, 52
universities, study of international relations in, 14, 59

Vardon, T., 60
Victoria, Queen of Great Britain, 36, 46
Vietnam, 34, 35, 56n., 86, 88, 89, 91, 92, 124, 136, 138, 139n., 140, 141, 142, 164, 174
Vogel, R., 50n.
Voice and Vision, 132
Vote Office, 49
Votes and Proceedings, 49

Wade, E. C. S., 37n.
Walker, P. C. G. *M.P.*, 73, 101, 126
Waller, I., 132n.
Walston, Baron, 97
war:
declaration of, and royal prerogative, 36, 37–40
and unanimity, 162
in U.S.A., 17, 30n., 38
Parliament refuses to support, 19, 39
see also First World War; Second World War
Warbey, W. N. *M.P.*, 47, 56n., 110, 139n.
Ward, Sir Adolphus W., 98n.
Watt, D. C., 142 n.
Webster, Sir Charles K., 174
Western European Union, 53n.
Western Germany *see* Germany, Federal Republic of
Wheare, K. C., 149
whip:
resignation of, 120, 121, 141
withdrawal of, 122, 125, 138
Whips, 55, 77, 78, 118, 122, 137, 138, 141–2, 148

190